# THE CARMEL MISSION

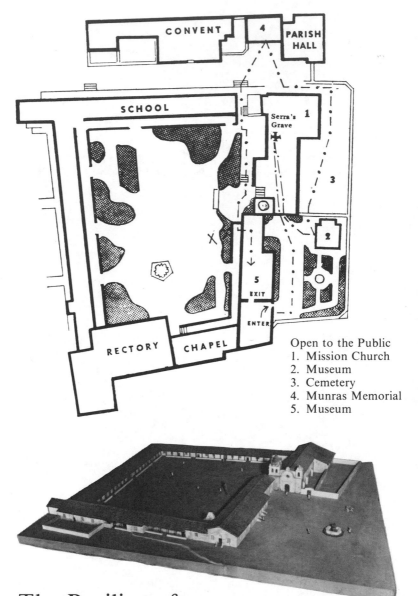

CONVENT

4

PARISH
HALL

SCHOOL

Serra's
Grave

1

3

2

5
EXIT

ENTER

RECTORY   CHAPEL

Open to the Public
1. Mission Church
2. Museum
3. Cemetery
4. Munras Memorial
5. Museum

# The Basilica of
# Mission San Carlos Borromeo

# THE CARMEL MISSION
## FROM FOUNDING TO REBUILDING

## by Sydney Temple

with
### Marguerite M. Temple
as Editorial Assistant

8 East Olive Ave., Fresno, California
A Division of Book Publishers, Inc.

Front Cover photograph and others in the text by
Marguerite M. Temple
Back cover photograph by Carlos Corredor
Other illustrations used by permission of:
Colton Hall Collection
Downie Collection
*Glimpses of California and the Missions*, by H. H. Jackson
Hathaway Collection
Huntington Library
Mayo Hayes O'Donnell Library
*Mission San Carlos Borromeo*, by Fr. Z. Engelhardt
*Mission to Paradise*, by K. M. King
Mission Trails Association
Monterey County Library
Museo Casa Junípero Serra
Museo Naval, Madrid
Pacific Grove Museum
Maps drawn by Joe Pierre

Valley Publishers
8 East Olive Avenue
Fresno, California 93728

Library of Congress No. 79-57168
ISBN 0-913548-71-5

*To Harry Downie*

*Supervisor of the reconstruction of
the Mission San Carlos Borromeo
who has contributed so much to this
volume that he is almost co-author.*

# About the Author

SYDNEY TEMPLE, a graduate of U.C.L.A., wrote his doctoral thesis at Columbia University on William White, chaplain of the Continental Congress in Philadelphia. He was later the Curator of Revolutionary and Civil War manuscripts at the College of William and Mary in Williamsburg, Virginia. After teaching at the University of Massachusetts, Huron College of the University of Western Ontario, and the University of Hawaii, he retired to Carmel in 1976.

MARGUERITE TEMPLE is the middle of three generations of native born Californians, her father and son also having been born in California. She didn't leave the state until her marriage to Sydney Temple, after which they lived in Illinois, Nevada, California, Maryland, Connecticut, Massachusetts, Ontario and Hawaii, as well as shorter times in Oxford, London and Jerusalem. She is a member of the Friends of Photography which has its international headquarters in the Sunset Cultural Center in Carmel.

# Contents

# List of Illustrations

# ONE

# The Padre-Presidente at the Carmel Mission

he most notable resident that Carmel, California, has ever had was born on the twelfth of November, 1713, in Petra, a small village in the middle of the island of Mallorca. Petra, meaning 'rock' in Greek, must have been the name given to the place by the Greek settlers who arrived on the Spanish peninsula and neighboring isles in the seventh century before the birth of Christ. Miguel José Serre, who was later to make Carmel the center for the civilizing of all California, may truly be said to have sprung from the Rock of Mallorca.

The parents of Miguel José, Antonio and Margarita Serre, kept the spelling of their surname according to the Mallorcan dialect as spoken on the island. The word *serre* in the Mallorcan dialect, which is *serra* in the Catalonian dialect and *sierra* in Castilian Spanish, is the word for 'a saw' and a handsaw is to be seen on the coat of arms of the family. This is, of course, from the same Latin root as the English verb 'serrate'. In popular Spanish idiom a mountain range came to be referred to as 'Sierra' because of the sawtooth appearance of a series of mountain peaks. The boy who was to adopt the Catalonian form of the word for his surname, Serra, was destined to become a man to match the Sierra, as the mountain ranges of California are still known.

Miguel José Serra grew up in the house in which he was born, Number 6 Barracar Street in Petra, and began his studies at the nearby Franciscan Friary of San Bernardino. The house at Number 6 was bought by the Rotary Club of Palma de Mallorca in 1932 and presented to the City of San Francisco. It is now administered by the Society of California Pioneers and is open daily. A native Californian born in San Francisco, Harry C. Hyer, is the Director of this Museo Casa Junípero Serra. Two doors away is another museum, known as "The Serra Museum," which was opened there in 1959. For those who would make a pilgrimage to Serra's birthplace there is bus service from the railway station at Palma several times a day, and a holiday resort, Porto Cristo, is only a half hour's drive away.

At the age of fifteen Miguel José moved on to the Lullian University in Palma, the school that was named for the poet and missionary, Raymond Lull. In Palma he joined the Franciscan Order, donning the habit of the long grey robe of unbleached wool which he was to wear for the rest of his life. He took the name Junípero (pronounced in Spanish Hoo-née-pay-row) after a Brother Juniper who had been a close friend and devoted follower of St. Francis, the founder of the order. Brother Juniper is said to have tried to outdo the founder in his ministrations to the poor; one story has it that he was once caught stripping the gold lace from the altar cloth with the intention of selling it and buying bread for the poor. Nothing in the larders of the community was safe from Brother Juniper's hands, we are told, if there were a hungry mouth anywhere in Assisi. Junípero Serra had taken an appropriate name, for in his later dealings with the Natives of California he certainly exhibited the character of his namesake. When Serra chose the name Junípero he was five feet two inches tall and was never to grow any taller. One would have thought that to

Fray Junípero Serra's birthplace at No. 6 Barracar Street, Petra,
Mallorca. (Museo Casa Junípero Serra in Petra)

be rather short for a juniper, but this juniper proved to be tall enough to cast a lasting shadow over all of California, once root was taken by the Rio Carmelo. And it was in that shade that civilization was to develop in California.

Fray Junípero Serra was ordained to the priesthood before he reached the canonical age and was appointed to the chair of Philosophy at Lullian University when he was only twenty-three. Two of his students at the University, Francisco Palóu and Juan Crespí, who were only a little younger than Serra, also entered the Franciscan Order and were to be his lifelong companions in the missionary activities in the New World. Fray Palóu, who was Serra's first biographer, told how he and his teacher declared their intention to become missionaries at the same time. Palóu wrote that one day as they were sitting together in Palma he declared to Serra, "I have a great wish that I have never told you," and continued, "I have long dreamed of going to the New World as a missionary." At this, according to the biographer, Junípero jumped from his chair with tears in his eyes, stating, "My prayers have been answered! How could you guess that I, too, would like to go to the New World?"

Stories of the exploits of the Spanish explorers in America were much talked about in Palma among the Franciscan Fathers, and New Spain (Mexico) beckoned the missionary minded. Three days after Easter in 1749 Fr. Serra, at the age of thirty-six, with his young friend Fr. Palóu embarked on the first leg of the trip, from Palma to Malaga on the mainland of Spain. Sailing then on a small coastal vessel around to Cadiz, they joined other Brothers gathered there to begin their journey to the land across the sea.* When it developed that five of those who had planned to go had reconsidered at the sight of the great waves breaking on the shore there, Fr. Serra reported

---

*A document in the Achiv de Indias, Seville, Spain, describes Serra when in Cadiz in 1749 as "thirty-six years old, of medium height, swarthy, dark eyes and hair, scant beard."

to the Brother in charge that Fr. Juan Crespí and several others among the Franciscan Friars at Palma were anxious to join the missionary groups. It was agreed that these others would follow in the next ship, and Serra was assured that Crespí would soon join him and Palóu in their overseas venture.

After a ninety-nine-day voyage from Cadiz, the ship bearing the missionaries reached Vera Cruz in New Spain. There they found that the Viceroy of New Spain had sent mules to bear the missionaries on the 270-mile journey over the 7,000-foot high mountains through tangled tropical jungles, across arid plains and over great unbridged rivers. Though the Franciscan rule forbidding the Brothers to ride when they could walk had been waived in this case, Serra wished to make the journey to Mexico City on foot, as St. Francis had always made his journeys. With one Franciscan Brother he started the long walk, taking no food but planning to go from one primitive *pueblo* to the next, "trusting in heaven to provide for their needs."

The journey was not to be without incident. One night, as the two were sleeping in the jungle, an insect bit Serra on the foot and he scratched at the bite in the night. Whether from the poison of the bite or the infection brought on by the scratching, the next morning the foot was greatly swollen. This made the remainder of the journey extremely difficult for Serra. The wound was never to heal completely, and the foot caused him pain and difficulty in walking as long as he lived.

On New Year's Day, 1750, Fr. Serra, with the help of his companion, hobbled into the Franciscan College of San Fernando in Mexico City. At that time this was the largest and finest city of the North American continent. In comparison, New York, Boston and Philadelphia were small towns, for the prosperity brought on by the riches from the silver and gold mines had attracted the crowds and produced the grandeur of this Spanish city in the New World. The streets were lined with many large stone 'palace-like' structures built by the Grandees who had come from Spain to make their fortunes from the mines. (With the recent discovery in Mexico of vast reserves of oil there is promise that this 'black gold' will again bring riches to Mexico City. Yet the poor within that city and the *peons* in the Mexican countryside continue to be gripped by the abject poverty in which Fr. Serra found the '*pobre Indios*' for whom he cared so greatly.)

Sketch of the main square of Mexico City in the eighteenth century. The Cathedral is in the background, the Viceroy's Palace to the right.

At the College of San Fernando Frs. Serra, Palóu and Crespí received their missionary training and for the next nineteen years were involved in the Franciscan missionary activity in New Spain which radiated from the college. It was in this period that Fr. Serra became in his preaching a sort of 'Savonarola of the New World'. The contrast between the ostentatious luxury of the upper classes in Mexico City and the desolate lives of the natives of the land moved him to lash out at the injustices of the situation. A recent biographer of Serra, Kenneth M. King of the Franciscan Order, has described his preaching at that time: "Like St. Jerome, Serra would beat his bare breast with a heavy stone, holding high the crucifix in the other hand, and calling for repentance. To illustrate the pains of hell he would hold a burning torch to his chest until the smell of scorched flesh alarmed the congregation. This burning zeal had an irresistible appeal both to the rich and to the poor; intellectuals were attracted to the wealth of knowledge and scholarship which had been developed in his university days; the rich were awed by the sincerity he showed; the *Indios* admired his ability to bear pain unflinchingly, for such stoicism was regarded among them as one of the most laudable 'virtues.'"*

At the age of fifty-six Fr. Juípero Serra was to begin the venture by which he shall always be remembered: the bringing of Christianity and with it civilization to California from a center on the Carmel River. When the Franciscans took over the Jesuit Missions of Baja California, Serra was appointed the Padre-Presidente to be in charge of them. At the same time he was commissioned by Don José de Gálvez, the Visitador-General of New Spain, to take the lead in establishing missions in the region to the north which was to be known as 'Nueva California,' New California.

On May 16, 1769, the day after the first Sunday of Pentecost, Fr. Serra joined the group under the command of the Governor of Baja California, Don Gaspar de Portolá, as a part of the first overland expedition to the fabled Bay of Monterey about which Vizcaino had written so glowingly after his visit there 167 years earlier. Previously two packetboats had sailed out of San Blas carrying extra supplies for the expedition, and a first land division had gone ahead to break the trail and mark out the path. Fr. Crespí was with that first land division. The land parties and the ships were to rendezvous at the port of San Diego Alcala.

On the march north Serra's foot became so inflamed that

---

*Kenneth M. King, *Mission to Paradise*, pp. 13-14.

A sketch of the portrait of Serra made in Mexico City.

Portolá ordered him to leave the expedition and to remain at the Mission San Francisco Xavier which was nearby. The padre refused to halt and, looking for some relief, noticed that one of the muleteers was rubbing an ointment made of hot tallow and herbs on the saddle galls of one of the mules. Over the protests of the muleteer Serra insisted that he should try the ointment on his inflamed leg and foot. It worked so well that it was called a "miracle," and Serra was able to continue the walk to their destination.

It was at the next place reached, the Mission Guadalupe, that Serra was offered a native lad of fifteen to be his personal attendant. This companion, Juan Evangelista, was to be highly valuable to the padre in the future, for he was quick to learn the language of other natives and served as the first interpreter for the missionaries in California. As Fr. Serra met the 'gentiles' on the way, as unconverted natives were called, he was shocked to see the men going "as naked as Adam in Paradise," but was pleased to find that the women were modestly clothed in their tule skirts and fur capes. Of the natives in Nueva California he wrote in his diary: "Their grace, vigour, friendliness and gaiety are charming. They have given us fish and mussels, and have danced for our entertainment. Our mules terrify them and nothing will induce them to approach one." Later, however, when the natives lost their fear of the four-footed beasts of burden, they would cause trouble by teasing the mules and frightening them.

By summer the two ships and both land parties had arrived in San Diego, though most of the sailors on the ships were ill. Nevertheless, on July 16 the first mission in Nueva California was established by the Padre-Presidente. Taking the name of the port at which it was located, this first mission was dedicated to the Franciscan Lay Brother, St. Didacus (Diego) of Alcala, for whom Viscaino had named the port when he sailed by on St. Didacus Day, November 12, 1602. A presidio was established there and some of the soldiers left to guard the new mission, while the remainder continued north with Portolá as he sought to find a land route to Monterey Bay, where the central settlement of Alta California was to be located.

Fr. Crespí accompanied this group while Fr. Serra remained at the new mission. In his diary Crespí reported that as they passed by the place that they named *Nuestra Señora la Reina de los Angeles* (Our Lady the Queen of the Angels) they experienced an earthquake, the first recorded in California. In the region they also saw for the first time "a strange black liquid bubbling out of the earth" which they called 'bitumen'. This was the same "strange black liquid" that Alexander the Great had noticed on his way through Persia two thousand years earlier but which was not to become the lifeblood of civilization for another century and a half. The 'bitumen springs' which Crespí described in his diary are still to be seen at what are now called the La Brea Pits in Los Angeles, from which the remains of mastodons, sabre-tooth tigers and other prehistoric animals have been recovered.

Sketch of Rumsen natives probably made by José Cardero, who visited Carmel with the Malaspina expedition in 1791. (Museo Naval, Madrid)

Though Portolá did reach Monterey Bay and the Carmel River, planting large crosses on the shore at both places, the supply ship was driven back by adverse winds so that, without fresh supplies, the Governor was forced to retrace his steps to San Diego. On their return trip they subsisted on seeds given to them by friendly natives and the meat of their pack mules. At the San Diego Mission Portolá found that food was dangerously low because no other supply ships had arrived from San Blas in his absence. He decided to close the mission and abandon the whole venture, returning overland to Baja California. At this time, according to Crespí's diary, Serra vowed that "although all turn back, yet will I remain here with my beloved Fray Juan Crespí." This echoed the sentiment that Serra had written to his parents on leaving Mallorca for the New World, "My watchword will be 'Always to go forward and never to turn back.'" At Serra's urging Portolá agreed to a nine-day wait before abandoning the San Diego Mission while the Franciscan Fathers conducted a Novena of Prayer for the arrival of the supply ships. In a "miraculous manner" the packetboat *San Antonio* came into view on the ninth day. With the expedition reprovisioned, plans were made to proceed again by land and by sea to Monterey Bay.

The condition of his foot and leg forced Serra to board the *San Antonio* for the trip north while Crespí again went with Governor Portolá on the 460-mile journey by foot. The land party arrived back at the bay and the Carmel River ahead of the ship, which again was fighting the contrary winds along the rocky shore. There Crespí found that the cross erected as a signal to the ships on the bluff above the river had already prepared the natives for conversion. The gifts of food that were found beside the cross and the arrows stuck into the ground around it showed that the natives recognized some religious significance. This was borne out by witness made to Fr. Crespí, who recorded it in his diary: "When the neophytes spoke Spanish well enough to be understood, they on various occasions explained that the first time they saw our men they noticed that every one wore on his breast a small glittering cross; that when the Spaniards had gone away and left this large cross on the shore, they dreaded to approach the sacred sign because at night they would see it surrounded by brilliant rays which would even dispel the darkness; that the cross appeared to grow larger so as to reach the skies; that in the daytime, when it stood in its natural size without the rays, they would approach it and offer meat, fishes and mussels in order to enlist its favor, lest it should harm them, and that, when to their amazement they saw that the cross did not consume those things, they would offer their plumes and arrows in token of their desire to be at peace with the people who planted it there."

Portolá's cross as it appeared to the natives. (Photo by Marguerite Temple, prepared by Filmcraft, Carmel)

On May 31, 1770, one week after the land party had arrived and set up camp by the Carmel River, the lookouts who had been left on Point Pinos sighted the *San Antonio*. On June 3, the first Sunday of Pentecost, the Padre-Presidente together with Fr. Crespí and in the name of the Apostolic College for the Propagation of the Faith declared a mission to be founded on the shores of Monterey Bay under the patronage of San Carlos Borromeo. Carlos Borromeo (1538–84), who had been the Cardinal Bishop of Milan, and famous as a teacher and humanitarian, was canonized at the beginning of the seventeenth century. Gálvez had given instructions that the mission at Monterey be dedicated to San Carlos Borromeo because he was the patron saint of King Charles III.

Governor Portolá returned on the *San Antonio* to the capital at Loreto, leaving Lieutenant Pedro de Fages in command at Monterey. It is reported that when the messengers sent by Portolá arrived in Mexico City with the news of the founding of the central mission for Nueva California, there was great rejoicing at the news of the "conquering of Califor nia." Crowds are said to have gathered in the street. Banners appeared and church bells pealed. In celebration of the event Visitador-General Gálvez arranged for ten more missionaries to be sent from the Franciscan college for the founding of more missions in California.

Fr. Serra soon realized that the location of the mission adjacent to the presidio on Monterey Bay was not ideal and applied to Gálvez for permission to move it to the Carmel River location, six miles to the south. The proposed move was desirable for two reasons: to have the native converts farther away from the soldiers of the presidio and to locate the mission in a place suited to the agriculture which must be developed to support the expected number of neophytes.

The problems with the soldiers resulted from the fact that there were in California few of the Catalonian Volunteers, the highly trained and well disciplined troops from Spain. The 'leather-jacket' soldiers in California were from a much less disciplined group which included many of the jailbirds who had been allowed their liberty on condition that they go to

California. They had caused trouble in Baja California and would certainly do the same at the new mission.

Both Vizcaino and Portolá had chosen to stay at the river rather than on the bay when they had come to this region, so the move of the mission to this more attractive area seemed inevitable. Fr. Kenneth M. King in his biography of Fr. Serra, *Mission to Paradise*, expresses the situation well when he writes that the Padre-Presidente "was sensitive to the beauty of nature and there is hardly a more beautiful spot to be found on earth than the green vale of Carmelo." We who live here would not argue with that. When permission arrived in May of 1771 in a letter from Gálvez brought on the *San Antonio*, Fr. Serra lost no time in making preparations for the move. On the same ship came the ten Franciscan Friars sent by Gálvez. The Padre-Presidente made plans immediately for the founding of more missions in California.

Though this is the story of Carmel and this chapter concerns the life of Junípero Serra at Carmel, the first nine missions in California are a part of the story, for they were established from Carmel by this amazing man. As Monterey was the center of government for Nueva California, Carmel was the center of the religious energy which was to civilize the area. The story of the Franciscan missions from San Diego to San Francisco is the story of the influence of those who lived and worked at the Mission San Carlos Borromeo de Carmelo.

By the summer of 1771 Serra had chosen the site for his mission on the north side of the Carmel River. On a little hill which was near some established native *rancherias* and overlooked the broad valley of Rio Carmelo, the construction for the central mission of California was begun. Moving into a hut on the site, Fr. Serra himself directed the construction by forty neophytes who had come from the missions of Baja California, three soldiers and five sailors. He first erected a great cross around which daily services were held until a building was ready to be used as a chapel. This cross was still standing prominently in the midst of the mission buildings when Vancouver visited there in 1792. The stones about the base and the remains of wood from the cross shaft were discovered by Harry Downie in 1938 as he was in the process of the rebuilding of the mission buildings. On its original site he erected a reconstruction of Serra's cross, which can be seen today outside the sarcophagus room of the mission.

Sketch of the Mission San Carlos Borromeo, the second mission founded by Serra, with the native *rancheria* beyond Serra's cross. (Museo Naval, Madrid)

The activity in building the new quarters for his beloved San Carlos Mission did not consume all of Serra's energy, which was also directed toward the evangelization of all the natives of California. Leaving the construction work under the supervision of the overseer whom he had trained, he went over to the Salinas River and up into the Santa Lucia Mountains to find a location for the next mission to be founded. In a fertile mountain valley some seventy-five miles from the sea and on the route between San Diego and Carmel, the padre found his site. It is reported that once he had chosen the site he hung a bell from a tree and began to ring it loudly. A lone native came at the sound of the bell, we are told, then ran away. Soon, however, he returned, bringing others, and the first congregation of the new mission was assembled. The Mission San Antonio de Padua was dedicated to Anthony, the Franciscan who had preached so effectively at Padua against the heretics

A sketch showing Fr. Serra ringing a bell at the site of the Mission San Antonio de Padua and one native responding to the call.

of northern Italy. This, the third of the missions in Nueva California, was established on July 14, 1771, with Frs. Pieras and Sitzer in charge. These padres soon began the development of irrigation canals which today form the basis for the irrigation system which is in use on the farms of the area.

The Padre-Presidente then sent word to San Diego that two friars were to be sent out from there to found another mission in the southern region. The site chosen was near the place called Nuestra Senora la Reina de los Angeles and in September of 1771 the Mission San Gabriel Archangel was established, the fourth mission established under Serra. Unfortunately the military commander of the presidio at San Diego sent soldiers to the mission soon after its founding, presumably to protect the padres. The 'leather jackets' treated the natives in such a manner that there was an early uprising near the mission; there were no converts at San Gabriel for several years and the mission itself was in constant danger of attack.

But at San Carlos Borromeo the first baptism of a native neophyte took place in December, before the move was made to the Rio Carmelo location.

The first buildings at Rio Carmelo, like those in Monterey, were built of logs stuck in the ground to form a solid wall with other logs laid across the top. On these horizontal logs there was a mat of sticks and a covering of turf to form the primitive (and not very waterproof) roof. The move to the river location was made on Christmas Eve, 1771. In his biography of Serra, Fr. Palóu states that the first buildings there "consisted of one room for a chapel, to which were added a dwelling of four rooms, and a larger room for a granary, besides a house for keeping the boys and a kitchen. All these structures were of wood and had a flat roof, and all were surrounded by a stockade. At one corner of the stockade a house was built to serve as a room for the guards and within sight some corrals for the mules and cattle were erected."

Juan Evangelista, who had been Serra's attendant since joining him in Baja California, soon began to understand the language of the Rumsens and was able to serve as an interpreter for the padres. The natives learned to understand and speak Spanish more readily than did the padres master the native dialects. A picture of the Padre-President in his relationship with the natives is included in Fr. Palóu's account: "When the pagans visited the venerable Father and there was seldom a day on which they failed to do so, attracted by curiosity or by the little presents he gave them, the first thing he would do was to make the sign of the cross on them with his own hands then he had them venerate the holy cross. After the conclusion of these holy ceremonies he would regale them either with food of boiled wheat or corn he ordered for them, or with *atole*, mush made of those grains, or with beads and trinkets as much as he could, in this way learning from them their language ... He taught the neophytes to salute everybody with the pious *Amor a Dios* (Love to God). The custom spread in such a way that even the pagans would utter the salutation not only to the Fathers but to every Spaniard. It would touch the hardest heart to hear the pagans meeting their companions or Spaniards on the road saluting with the words *Amor a Dios.*"

The first livestock arrived at the new mission location while the buildings were being erected. A boar and a sow with four pigs were herded over from Monterey while nine cows with calf, two yearling heifers and six heifer calves were driven up from San Diego—the normal allowance for a new mission. To these was added a bull that was sent as a personal gift from the San Diego padres. Another thirty-six head of cattle destined for the mission on San Francisco Bay were later to be kept at Carmel. They were to increase greatly in number before the mission dedicated to the founder of the Franciscan Order was established. It is from these small herds that most of the thousands of head of cattle in California are descended.

Though California had been 'conquered' without warfare except for the uprising at the San Gabriel Mission, a new sort of trouble came upon the enterprise in 1772, the year after the establishment of the Carmel mission. There arose the real possibility that all the missions in Nueva California would have to be abandoned and all the missionaries and soldiers would have to start the long walk south. The missions as well as the presidios of California were entirely dependent upon the ships which came from Baja California, for the herds were not large enough to provide food and the crops had not yet been established. As they were converted the natives came to live at the mission *rancherias* where they were fed and cared for; at the presidios, in addition to the troops, there were the native neophytes brought as laborers from Baja California. Ship captains feared to sail to San Diego and Monterey in the winter because of the gales experienced along the shores, and those who did attempt the passage north were often driven back. In the winter of 1771–72 no ships had arrived at all.

In March word came from the south that supplies at San Diego and San Gabriel were nearly exhausted. Within a short time Fr. Crespí left Carmel with a pack train loaded with 2,400 pounds of flour for the southern missions. This left the San Carlos Mission and the Monterey Presidio short of supplies, but Serra felt that with the help of the natives, things would be all right until a ship should arrive. The chief of the Rumsen tribe was a good friend of the mission and helped by having his people bring gifts of deer and antelope as well as bags of seeds and *pinole* whenever they could. Yet by summer the situation had become desperate, as Fr. Serra wrote to Fr. Palóu, who was Director of the Missions in Baja California: "The principal supporters of our people are the pagan *Indios*. Through their sympathy we live as God wills, though the milk from the cows and some vegetables from the garden have been the chief subsistence—but both sources are becoming scarce." (And in 1976-77 some of us complained about the inconveniences that we experienced as a result of the drought!)

Captain Fages of the Monterey Presidio, in order to save the situation, took a contingent of soldiers on a hunting expedition to a valley some 50 leagues (140 miles) to the south which was famous as a haunt of bears. The valley had been named *La Cañada de los Osos* (The Valley of the Bears) by Portolá after his company had come upon a troop of bears there which had been fought off with difficulty after one horse had been killed by the beasts. Fages was successful in the hunt, sending twenty-five loads of jerked bear meat to the mission and keeping enough to provide for the presidio. This, with four loads of seed harvested by the natives at the Mission San Antonio Padua, bought time until a ship should arrive.

Father Serra went south with Fages and used the time to advantage while the soldiers were making their haul of bear meat. Continuing his plan to fill California with missions, even in the face of adversity, he used the place and the occasion to found a fifth mission. On the first of September in 1772 the

Mission San Luis Obispo Tolosa (St. Louis, Bishop of Tou-louse) was formally established in *La Cañada de los Osos* by the Padre-Presidente. This mission, which was approximately halfway between San Diego and Carmel, provided another station on what would someday be known as *El Camino Real* (The Royal Highway), which would link together the chain of California missions. At the same time Serra sought to estab-lish a sixth mission on the mainland across from the Channel Islands, between San Luis Obispo and San Gabriel, but Captain Fages refused his permission. It was to be another ten years before the Mission San Buenaventura was founded.

Proceeding south to San Diego, Serra found that the packetboat *San Antonio* had arrived there with a plenitude of supplies for the five missions.His joy was short-lived, however, when Captain Perez refused to sail his ship north against the contrary winds and gave orders to unload all the cargo at San Diego. After much heated argument the padre was able to convince the sea captain that it would be impossible to trans-port all the supplies the 170 leagues (approximately 450 miles) over the rugged Santa Lucia Mountains. The *San Antonio* left San Diego then and reached Monterey on September 27 with the life-saving supplies.

While the famine at the California missions had been allayed, the letters brought on the *San Antonio* brought news of disasters of a different sort to threaten the California enter-prise. In 1771 two of the strongest promoters of the California Project had been called back to receive honors and positions of importance in Spain, and had been replaced by men who were doubtful of the value of this far-flung adventure. Portolá was relieved as the Governor of California by one Matias de Armona who, from the capital in Loreto, issued orders that no new missions should be established in Nueva California. He called such activity "not only foolish but downright wicked" in that ill defended frontier—there were just forty-three soldiers in all of Nueva California in 1770 while three years later the number had only increased to sixty. Gálvez had left Mexico City for Spain and the new Viceroy was Antonio Bucareli, who was ready to take the advice of the new Governor of California. Learning of the new situation, the Padre-Presidente, small in stature but large in determination, decided to take the case for the California missions directly to the new Viceroy in Mexico City.

He arrived in Mexico City on the sixth of February to find that in that very month Bucareli had decided that the whole California enterprise should be abandoned because of the tremendous difficulty and ever-increasing cost of keeping those distant outposts supplied. Serra set out at once to convince the new Viceroy that the mission to the natives of Nueva California was of greatest value as the best means to 'conquer' a large and valuable land for the Spanish crown. He summarized his arguments for the continued support for the California missions and presidios in a *Representación* of thirty-two clauses which he presented to Bucareli in person, appearing in a condition which was described as "old, infirm, uncouth and shabby" by an observer.

In this appeal the Padre-Presidente did not simply argue for a continuaton of the *status quo*, but made specific requests for improvements. Among these was an appeal that carpenters and blacksmiths be sent to the missions with the same pay and rations as the soldiers and that married soldiers and artisans be sent as the first step in the colonization of California. He reported that the natives were amazed to see only men arrive among them and had asked if marriage were unknown among the Spaniards. He argued that the country would never be a part of Spain until Spanish children were born there. He also suggested that cleared land and livestock be offered to any Spaniard who married a baptized native woman, thus establishing a self-supporting population for California.

Serra was especially concerned that the padres be given full control of the missions, which had been experiencing trouble with the military commanders, and that the neophytes be completely under the control of the missionaries. But he did not omit detailed requests. He appealed for the consideration of the return to Spain of eight soldiers at Monterey who had asked him to carry their petition to the Viceroy. He asked that more vestments and altar furnishings be sent for the existing missions and those that were yet to be established, as well as more bells, "especially those cast in Mexico City, which have a graceful shape and mellow tone."

While Serra's representation was being considered in Mexico City the missionary activity in California was undergoing a change. The Viceroy had ordered that the missions of Baja California be handed over to the Dominican Order, a change which the Franciscans welcomed, for their main interest was now in Nueva California. Fr. Palóu, who had been in charge of the southern missions, now moved to Carmel and became the acting Padre-Presidente in Serra's absence. He was accompanied by Fr. Francisco de Lasuén, who would eventually be Fr. Serra's successor and would be instrumental in the extension of the mission chain until El Camino Real was completed in the nineteenth century.

At the Carmel mission Fr. Palóu started the building of a new church. The original mud-roofed structure was proving to give inadequate protection from winter rains. The new church, 110 feet long, was built of logs and planks with a tule-thatched roof. The herd of livestock there was enlarged when Captain Fages sent over from the presidio four brood mares, three in foal, a stallion, six work horses, fourteen mules and a burro. The vegetable patch was enlarged by Palóu, who was an expert gardener. The magnificent lettuce he raised in the mission garden was the forerunner of that produced on the extensive farms of the Salinas Valley today, and from Palóu's artichokes have come the plants still producing in the Carmel Valley and throughout the region, giving the village of Castroville, north of Monterey, the title "the artichoke center of the world."

Back in Mexico City the plea that had been made to the Viceroy was bringing the desired results. A new manager was appointed to handle the supplies to be sent north from San Blas and work was renewed on the ships being built there. It was ordered that the missionaries were hereafter to have full control of the missions and that they were to be in the position *in loco parentis* to the converted neophytes. Though the capital of California was to remain at Loreto in the south, a new Commandante, Captain Fernando Rivera y Moncado, was appointed for Nueva California, and was instructed to recruit soldier-settlers and their families to take north with him. Serra had convinced Viceroy Bucareli that from the settlements in California great cities might someday grow, and for the first time a definite plan was made for the establishment of pueblos there. Pending was a petition from Don Juan Bautista de Anza for permission to scout a route from Sonora in northern New Spain (now in New Mexico) to California, by which settlers and livestock might be taken overland. The consideration of the petition had been postponed by the *Junta* with little hope of favorable action, before Serra arrived in Mexico City. Now the Viceroy ordered that such an expedition should be undertaken for the overland supplying of California and de Anza began at once to make his preparations.

Serra was sent back to Carmel with generous provisions, including, at his request, five bales of cloth for garments for the natives. A second friar accompanied him on the return journey, as well as a surgeon with his family and six mechanics of the sort that the Padre-Presidente had requested. On January 24, 1774 the party sailed north from San Blas on the new ship *Santiago*, the very ship on which Serra had seen construction halted as he passed through a year earlier on his way to Mexico City. At San Diego Serra left the ship and continued the journey by land to Carmel in order to visit all the missions which had been established in Nueva California.

Anza arrived at the San Gabriel mission at about the same

time that Serra arrived in San Diego. Leaving Tubac in Sonora the previous September, Anza and his party had followed the Colorado River for a ways before cutting across the desert and making their way through the rough mountain passes to establish the overland route to California. They proceeded at once to Monterey and were received at the Carmel mission on April 20, 1774, in the midst of the second famine suffered there. Anza reported that the food at the mission consisted of milk and herbs without any bread and that the neophytes had all been sent away to find their own food of seeds and mussels. To spare the food supply the new arrivals stayed for only two days before starting their journey back.

Meeting Serra at the Mission San Luis Obispo on his return south, Anza was able to apprise the padre of the situation at Carmel, of which Palóu was to write: "The worst kind of famine that was ever endured in the regions around Monterey visited us. For eight months milk was the manna for all from the Commandante and the Fathers down to the least individual and I shared it with the rest. Thanks be to God, however, all are in good health. At this Mission of San Carlos for thirty-seven days we were without a tortilla or as much as a crumb of bread. The meals consisted of a gruel made of *garvanzos,* or beans, ground to flour with which milk was mixed. In the morning a little coffee took the place of chocolate." Another aspect of the privation is reported by Msgr. Culleton in his *"Indians and Pioneers of Old Monterey."* He states that "they did not mind the famine nearly as much as they did the absence of snuff, which seems to have run out in November '73."

Relief arrived on May 9, 1774, just two days before Serra reached Carmel, when the supply ship *San Antonio* sailed into Monterey Bay. We may be sure that this ship, which carried a full load of provisions for the presidio and the missions of the northern region, brought a plentiful supply of chocolate and snuff to restock the coffers. Aboard the *San Antonio* was the new Commandante, Don Fernando Rivera, as well as the first white women to arrive in California, listed as four matrons and three maidens. Also aboard were the physician who had come from Mexico City with Fr. Serra and three carpenters so badly needed for both their building skills and their contribution in the instruction of the natives.

The padres were attempting to make the mission self-sufficient by developing the crops in the valley. In 1774, 207 bushels of wheat, 250 bushels of maize and 45 bushels of beans were harvested, and in the next year the total had increased to 980 bushels, according to mission records. Oxen were trained to draw the primitive plow, made of two pieces of wood held together by leather thongs with an iron blade affixed to the leading edge. Natives were learning to be plowmen, as they were learning to make adobe bricks, sun-dried blocks of clay, and to be carpenter's helpers. The acceptance of the mission by the natives was marked when chief Tatlum of the Carmel Rumsens was married to his wife in Christian ceremonies in 1775, both taking new Christian names.

It was also in that year, on September 29, 1775, that Anza set

A sketch made to illustrate the primitive plowing technique in the Carmel Valley. The mission is seen in the distance.

out again from Sonora, following the trail that he had established on his previous trip and this time bringing with him settlers for San Francisco. The party of 240 persons included 20 families of farmers and soldiers, all mounted on horseback. They brought with them 500 horses, 350 head of cattle and a pack train of 165 mules laden with household goods and agricultural tools, as well as supplies for the journey. Successfully negotiating the difficult trail over desert and mountains, they arrived at the San Gabriel mission on the fourth of January 1776.

At the San Gabriel mission they were met with news of the worst uprising among the natives which had been or was to be experienced in California. On December thirteenth of the previous year an attack had been made on the mission San Diego in which the buildings were destroyed and many persons killed including the padre, Fr. Jáyme (Haí-may). Commandante Rivera, who was hurrying south with thirteen soldiers to put down the uprising, was joined by Anza and his veteran border fighters. The combined forces were able to settle affairs at San Diego and to prevent a general revolt of the native population, though the Mission San Diego had to be abandoned temporarily and the building of the new mission buildings at San Juan Capistrano halted.

An insight into the faith of Junípero Serra and his undaunted determination to convert the natives of California can be gained from his reaction to this tragedy. Because he was convinced that martyrdom guaranteed an immediate entrance into heaven he saw death of Fr. Jáyme as a step forward. It is reported that when he heard of the massacre at San Diego he exclaimed, "Thank God! The blood of a martyr has fertilized the soil, and the conversion of the gentiles [the pagan natives] is made sure." He sent a message south with Rivera to be forwarded from San Diego to Mexico City, assuring the Viceroy that the Franciscans in California were not discouraged, but rather heartened after this setback.

Anza returned to his party at the Mission San Gabriel and proceeded to Monterey, arriving there on March 10, 1776. Leaving the large group at the presidio in Monterey, Anza and his chaplain, Fr. Pedro Font, accepted the invitation to stay at the mission. Like many before and after them, they found Carmel to be a delightful place to stay. Fr. Font included this description of the Carmel mission in his diary: "The Mission San Carlos de Carmelo is situated on a little elevation near the sea and close to the Carmel River which empties into a little bay called by Vizcaino the Puerto del Carmelo. It is an

The reenactment of the Anza trek from Sonora to San Francisco as the party passed Carmel on the two hundredth anniversary in 1976. (Courtesy of the Hathaway Collection)

excellent site with very fertile lands. The temperature is cold in a desirable way and very healthful, although somewhat foggy, as is the case on the whole coast. The mission has a rather spacious and well made church, although it is of palisades and tule for the most part, and it is somewhat adorned with paintings. Apart from it are three good sized rooms of adobe for the dwellings of the Fathers. Separate from it are a kitchen, forge and two or three rooms." In Fr. Font's account the Rumsen natives passed the 'B.O. test' and he was impressed with their appearance and fishing skill: "The Indios of this mission who already number 400 Christians appeared to me to be rather tractable, not so ugly, nor so ill-smelling as those of San Diego. They devote themselves to fishing, for at this place many good fish are caught. Besides the sardines, which are plentiful, there are also many good salmon which enter the river to spawn. Of this fish we ate almost every day while we were here. In short, although the rest of the missions are very good, this one seemed to me to be the best of all."

The steelhead salmon still go up from the Carmelo Bay when the river flows into the ocean in the winter rainy season and the fishing is very good at that time. Before dams were built upriver there was evidently an all-year flow of the river past the Mission San Carlos.

Fr. Font's graphic description of the garden plot is such as might be made of many gardens in the Carmel area today: "I went to take a walk through the garden, which is a stone's throw from the mission. It was a delight to see it so beautiful and full of vegetables, cared for by Father Palóu with such diligence that he spent all day working in it and had it very well laid out. It is square and all around it has a border of azaleas already in flower and the beds full of cauliflower, lettuce and other vegetables and herbs. And the finest thing about that country is that without irrigation all such vegetables are raised, than which there are no better in Mexico. Indeed one artichoke would ordinarily last from two to three days. They only water the plants by hand, throwing on each plant a gourdful of water after transplanting and this suffices."

The trek of the Anza party was reenacted in 1976, on the 200th anniversary, with riders taking turns as the route was followed from Tubac, Sonora to San Francisco, California, via the missions from San Gabriel to Carmel and on to the Mission Dolores on the great bay.

Captain Rivera, as Commandante, still refused permission for the movement of the settlers north to the bay so that Anza was forced to begin his return to Sonoma in April, leaving his group of unhappy settlers at Monterey. Before departing, however, he made a trip north to see what he called "the harbor of harbors" about which he then wrote prophetically, "I think that if it could be well settled like Europe, there would not be anything more beautiful in all the world, for it has the best advantages for founding on it a most beautiful city." Certainly the 'well settled' city of San Francisco has fulfilled Anza's prediction for it is generally known as "the most European of American cities."

It was not until the packetboat *San Carlos* arrived with definite orders that a presidio and mission should be established on the San Francisco Bay that Captain Rivera relented. On June 17, 1776 Lt. Commander José Joaquin Moraga, with Frs. Palóu and Cambon, led the settlers with their livestock to the bay, their provisions and equipment having gone ahead of them by ship. The Mission San Francisco de Asis (St. Francis of Assisi) was situated near the *Arroya de los Dolores* (Stream of Sorrows) by the entrance to the bay and came to be known popularly as the Mission Dolores. The building of the presidio was completed in September and the mission, the sixth in Nueva California, was dedicated on the ninth of October in the same year that the American Declaration of Independence was signed on the other side of the continent.

In November of that year trouble at the Mission San Luis Obispo led to an advantageous change in the construction of all the California missions. The buildings there, as at all the missions, had been built with a roof of tule rushes. When an enemy native shot a flaming arrow onto the roof all the buildings of the compound were burned except the chapel. Inspired by necessity, the padres devised a method of forming and baking tiles for a fireproof roof covering. It is said that the shape of the roof tiles was made as a native molded the wet clay around his shin. The same type of tiles is still used on the roofs of the Spanish style buildings in California.

It was at about that time that a neophyte rushed to the padres at the Carmel mission with a warning that the Ensens, ancient enemies of the Rumsens, were armed for battle and were coming up Los Laureles Canyon toward the mission. The mission guard was hurriedly sent to the presidio for help and a sergeant came over with a small squad of soldiers. The seven padres then in residence at the mission were ordered to spend the night in one room where they could be protected. But no attack was made and the Carmel record of unbroken peace with the natives was continued.

San Diego continued to be a trouble spot, however, even after the native uprising had been settled. When the mission there was attacked and Fr. Jáyme killed, the other padre in residence, Fr. Fuster, hid in a warehouse and so escaped injury. After the arrival of the soldiers Fr. Fuster gathered around him at the church the remaining neophytes, including one who had taken part in the insurrection and was now penitent. The trouble came when the native, named Carlos, was taken from the church and the padre's protection by Captain Rivera and placed in prison. For this breach of the rule of 'sanctuary' Fr. Fuster excommunicated the Commandante of Nueva California. The case was referred to the Padre-Presidente in Carmel and Serra ruled that the excommunication should hold until Carlos was released from prison. The Commandante refused to release him and the matter stood at an impasse between the church and the military authority.

A further cause for conflict between the two authorities in California came when Rivera ordered that the presidio in San Diego should be rebuilt but not the mission. Fr. Serra could not allow one of his missions to be abandoned without a struggle, so he sailed down to San Diego at once on the returning packetboat *San Antonio*. From there he sent urgent messages to the authorities in Mexico City, seeking rulings on the matters which were disturbing the California province. The order came back from Viceroy Bucareli by the next ship that the Mission San Diego Alcala should be rebuilt at once and that Carlos should be released from prison into the care of Fr. Fuster.

Work on the mission north of San Diego had been stopped after the San Diego attack, but now word came from Bucareli that the work there should be carried on. The building was completed in November of 1776, and the seventh mission founded by Serra was dedicated in the name of San Juan Capistrano (St. John of Capistran), the monk who had fought against the Ottoman Turks while still wearing his Franciscan garb. The adobe chapel, one of California's oldest buildings, is the one part of the original compound that survived the 1812 earthquake. It is the only building still standing in which Fr. Serra actually conducted services and administered the sacraments.

Next another mission was established on the San Francisco Bay, the eighth founded by Serra. This mission, on the western shore of the Bay, south of the mission San Francisco, was dedicated in January, 1777, to Santa Clara de Asis (St. Clare of Assisi), the founder of the Order of Poor Clares. In the middle of the nineteenth century the care of this mission was assigned to the Jesuits who established a college there, now the University of Santa Clara. None of the original mission building is in existence, but the modern chapel on the site is a faithful copy of the original church building that stood there. When Serra visited this mission in September, 1777, it is said that he covered the forty-five miles from the Santa Clara mission to the Mission Dolores in a day and a night of continuous walking. He was quoted as remarking on his first visit to the great bay, "Thanks be to God that you, Father Francis, with the Holy Cross of the procession of Missions, has reached the farthest boundary of the California continent. To go further we must go by boats." Missions were later built above the bay but this was as far north as Serra was to go.

In August of 1775 it had been ordered that the capital of 'the Californias' be moved to Monterey, but it was not until February 3, 1777, that Don Felipe de Neve arrived there to take his position as Governor. On the previous Christmas Day the *Reglamento* of de Neve had been published as a codified plan for California which put emphasis on the founding of *pueblos* (towns). The first secular civil authority under this plan for the 'peopling' of California was established in November of 1777 when San Jose was founded as a *pueblo* at the southern end of San Francisco Bay. Since this was the first town which was founded apart from a mission establishment, San Jose can make the claim to be "the first town of California."

In 1778 Fr. Serra received the document which authorized him to administer confirmation. The permission had been granted by the Pope in 1774 but it had taken four years for approval to be made by the king and Council and the word forwarded to the Padre-Presidente. The message arrived on June 17 and on the twenty-ninth of the month Serra confirmed ninety children with the chrism (holy oil) that had been blessed by the Bishop of Guadalajara. It is recorded that in his subsequent travels to the missions of California to administer confirmation he traveled 4,285 miles and confirmed more than two thousand people.

The affairs of the new nation on the eastern shores of the continent began to affect the western shores in 1779 when Spain joined France in supporting the thirteen colonies in their War of Independence against England. This was to cause a supply problem in California, as the ships were needed to transport war materials for the defense of the Philippine Islands against the British. But by this time the missions were better able to support themselves so their dependence upon the ships from the south was lessened. In that year Fr. Serra wrote to Fr. Lasuén, who was then in charge of the San Diego mission, that at the Mission San Carlos there had been harvested 1,660 bushels of wheat, 700 bushels of barley, 165 bushels of beans and 85 bushels of maize. The mission was even able to contribute in cash the equivalent of $106 to the Spanish war effort.

In November of 1781 Fr. Crespí assisted Fr. Serra in the cornerstone laying for a new church at the Santa Clara mission.* Within six weeks Fr. Crespí, the fellow Mallorcan who had been a lifetime companion of Fr. Serra in his work, died and was buried in the sanctuary of the new adobe church at the Mission San Carlos Borromeo de Carmelo. Two years later the Padre-Presidente was to say mass for the opening of the new church at Santa Clara just three months before his own death.

The last mission founded by Serra, Mission San Buenventura, had been planned by him and Visitador-General Gálvez in 1768, before the establishment of San Carlos at Carmel. The padres sent to supervise this mission had been available since 1771, but it was not until 1782 that Governor Fages gave permission for its founding. On Easter Day of that year the Padre-Presidente dedicated the mission to San Buenaventura, the thirteenth century Franciscan friar who was miraculously healed as a small child by St. Francis, who exclaimed, "O buono ventura!" (Oh good fortune).

By the end of 1783 the missions in California had attained the level of self-sufficiency that Serra had envisioned many years earlier. At the Carmel mission, enough land had been cleared to provide food for the 700 persons living at the mission and at the *rancheria* under its protection. An irrigation canal had been extended from the river to a pool for the keeping of fish, conveniently located near the mission enclosure. Cattle were at 520 head, and there were 82 horses, 20

---

*The cornerstone has been preserved and is in the museum at the University of Santa Clara.

mules and 25 pigs, in addition to the flocks of sheep at Carmel. Throughout the California mission system the livestock had now grown to a total of nearly 30,000 head while the annual harvests amounted to 30,000 bushels of grain and vegetables. The natives were by now trained plowmen, shepherds and *vaqueros*, horseback riding cattle herders, as well as blacksmiths and carpenters. Neophytes connected with the missions made adobe bricks of clay formed into cubes and dried in the sun, as well as the roof tiles which were baked in the kilns. Workshops at the nine missions provided most of what was needed, including rough furniture and simple agricultural tools.

An old Spanish map showing the chain of missions founded by Fr. Junípero Serra. San Carlos Mission is incorrectly titled "de Monterey" instead of "de Carmelo."

The Mission San Carlos Borromeo now consisted of the new adobe church in which Fr. Crespí was buried, a three-room priests' residence, two barns and thirty workshops. These were gathered around an open space in the center, with the native *rancherias* of the married neophytes extending outward. The *rancherias*, even those inhabited by unconverted natives, were very important in Serra's eyes. It was reported that on his last visit to all the California missions in 1874 the Padre-Presidente also visited twenty-one native *rancherias*. These visits were not in vain. In his last years Serra ministered to and baptized the chief of the Esselens, the traditional enemies of the Rumsens, marking the culmination of his years of activity among the members of that tribe. During the time that Serra had been the President of the California missions, six thousand natives had been baptized in the Province and he had confirmed about five thousand of these.

Serra's return from his last trip is described, perhaps somewhat romantically, by Fr. King in his *Mission to Paradise*: "As Serra approached San Carlos, the Indians, the Spanish soldiers and the whole motley population came forth to greet him, and lovingly led him back to his old quarters which had been thoughtfully refurnished against his return. He smiled thankfully, and told them simply: 'I have come home to die.'"

He called for his lifetime friend and companion, Fr. Palóu, to come from San Francisco to be with him in his last days. Palóu was able to tell him that Governor Fages had finally given his permission for the founding of a mission at Santa Barbara, a matter which had been of great concern to Fr. Serra. The dying padre still had one worry. There was a rumor that the Bishop of Sonora, who had authority over all California, was to turn over the Franciscan missions to the Dominican Order, as had been done in Baja California. Palóu could give him assurance that this was not to happen. The Franciscans did remain in charge of the missions until the secularization of them all, which was to come many years later.

And the Franciscan Order was never to lose Mission Santa Barbara once it was established, even at the time of the secularization of the missions. Santa Barbara has continued as a Franciscan establishment and is now the mother house of the Order on the Pacific Coast.

A reconstruction of the cell in which Junípero Serra lived and died as it may be seen today at the Mission San Carlos Borromeo in Carmel.

On August 28, 1784, four days before his seventy-ninth birthday, in the thirty-sixth year of his missionary work, Father Junípero Serra died at the Carmel mission. In compliance with his wishes, his body was interred next to his beloved Fr. Crespí in the sanctuary of the mission church. There their bodies remain, although the sanctuary is now in a stone church which was built on the site of the old adobe church.

A statue of Father Serra, one of the giants of California history, stands in Statuary Hall in our nation's Capitol to represent the State of California there. With a model of the

The statue of Father Junípero Serra in Statuary Hall in the Capitol Building in Washington, D.C. as one of the representative figures of California history.

Carmel mission church in the left hand and a cross held high in the right, the figure expresses well the contribution that Junípero Serra made to California.

On August 29, 1937, when Serra's reconstructed cell was dedicated at Mission San Carlos, the cause of his beatification was begun, a movement by which his name may be added to the roster of the Saints of the Church.

How shall one characterize the most notable resident of Carmel's history? Msgr. James Culleton, in his *Indians and Pioneers of Old Monterey*, has described him as "a strong-willed man, tenacious, logical, well-informed, pious and a good steady worker." He states that "it is hard to find a vein of humor in him, yet he must have smiled when he chose the name for the thousandth child baptized at Carmel, Millan Deogratias, 'A thousand, to-God-be-thanks.'" After Serra's death his old and ragged habit was cut into small pieces and distributed among the neophytes he loved; perhaps Millan Deogratias received a scrap of his robe as a relic of this holy man.

## Bibliographical Notes

Father Palóu had written of the life of Father Serra during his last years in California under the title, *Relacion Historica de la Vida y Apostolicas Tareas del Venerable Padre Junipero Serra*. This was published in Mexico City in 1787. After his retirement to the Franciscan headquarters in Mexico City he wrote *Noticias de la California* based on documents and notes that he had kept from the time that the Franciscans arrived at Loreto in Baja California. This was sent to Madrid but was not published until 1857 when it was included as four volumes of *Documentos para Historia de Mexico*. Both of these have appeared in English versions as translated in 1926 by

Professor Herbert E. Bolton, the latter under the title, *Historical Memoirs of New California* (University Press, Berkeley, California).

An English translation of Fr. Crespi's journals was offered the next year by Professor Bolton under the title, *Crespi, Missionary-Explorer, 1769-1774*. In 1930 appeared his *Anza's California Expedition* which includes the translation of Anza's diaries. In volume four of this five volume work is to be found the translation of the diary of Father Font.

A brief bibliography which provides the basis for further study of the missions and missionaries of California is to be found in *Mission to Paradise: The Story of Junipero Serra and the Missions of California* by Kenneth M. King, F.I.A.L. (Chicago: Franciscan Herald Press, 1956 and 1975), pp. 187-90.

# TWO

# Growth Years
# of the Carmel Mission
# and the Camino Real

century after the death of Junípero Serra there came to the ruined remnants of the San Carlos mission in Carmel the author of the book, *Ramona,* which then roused interest throughout the country in the history and fate of the California missions. In her record of that visit, Helen Hunt Jackson included a report that she heard at that time: "In the course of the next few months after his [Serra's] death more converts were baptized than in the whole three years previous; and it became at once the belief that his soul had passed directly into heaven, and that this great wave of conversions was the result of his prayers."* Whatever the origin of this story, certainly Serra's spirit did continue to influence the activities at Mission San Carlos Borromeo and throughout California through the leadership of Serra's successors in the Franciscan missionary enterprise.

Serra was succeeded for a short time by his lifelong friend and workmate, Fr. Francisco Palóu, who had been with him from his college days on Mallorca to the last days of his life at

---

* Helen Hunt Jackson, *Glimpses of California and the Missions (1883-1902),* p. 48.

the Carmel mission. Palóu at once applied for permission to retire to the Missionary College in Mexico City to write the history of the California missions and the biography of Junípero Serra. After Palóu sailed from Monterey another Padre-Presidente of the California missions was elected.

Fermín Francesco de Lasuén, from the Basque district of Spain, had been with Serra and Palóu when they sailed for New Spain with other Francsican Brothers in 1749. Lasuén had been in charge of the mission at Loreto in Baja California before coming north with Palóu when the Franciscans turned over the Baja California missions to the supervision of the Dominican Order. He first served at the San Gabriel and San Juan Capistrano missions in Alta California before taking charge of the San Diego mission, where he was when elected Padre-Presidente. Upon his election as the director of the California missions he moved to Carmel, the headquarters of all California missionary activity. It was during the term of Lasuén that San Carlos mission in Carmel had its greatest growth and the number of missions in California doubled. Within a year of taking over as Padre-Presidente at Carmel Lasuén was to establish the Mission Santa Barbara as the first of nine that he was to found as he strove to complete the task begun by Serra.

It is fortunate that during the period from 1784 to the end of the nineteenth century, the years of greatest growth, a series of foreign visitors came to the Carmel mission and left their impressions in words and pictures. By means of these records we are able to trace the development of the mission on the bank of the Carmel River and to see how it grew to its greatest prominence.

The first of these European visitors arrived in Monterey in 1786. Jean Francis Galoup de la Pérouse, a scientist and experienced seaman, had sailed from Brest on a worldwide voyage of exploration for the French government. Sailing around South America he visited several ports along the

Pacific shore before arriving in Monterey on September 18. A few days later he visited the Carmel mission.

There the expedition's artist, Gaspard Duché de Vancy, made a drawing of the reception given him there. The natives were drawn up on one side and the French soldiers on the other, and in the background were two of the seven church buildings that were to rise at the Carmel mission. On the right stands the building known as 'The Serra Adobe', built by Serra two years before his death. Therein were interred the bodies of Serra and Crespi, just inside the chancel.

La Pérouse reported in his journals that the interior of the church was ornamented with paintings copied from Italian

A sketch of the reception of La Pérouse at the Carmel mission made by de Vancy, the artist with the La Pérouse expedition. (Courtesy of the Downie Collection)

originals with representations of heaven and hell on the side walls. To the left of the Serra Adobe is to be seen the *Xacalon Grande* (Large Rough), built in 1778 as the last of the log-sided churches at Carmel. It was left to stand when the new adobe church was built and was being used for storage when this drawing was made. To the right is to be seen the customary ring of bells which was a part of the necessary equipment of a California mission. Fr. Lasuén is shown in the foreground as he received his French visitors but unfortunately only the back of his robe and a clear view of his tonsure are depicted. Perhaps the Franciscan Friar facing the artist was Fr. Noriega around whose administration of the natives trouble was later to arise.

Like visitors before and after him La Pérouse was enthusiastic about the countryside, commenting: "while his own native land had fertile soil, the fertility of the Pacific coast was something which no European farmer could imagine." He reported that, "The deer were almost tame and even the whales gambolled and spouted in the sea with a pleasant show of familiarity and a complete absence of fear." But his greatest enthusiasm was reserved for the missionaries and the generosity of the Spanish government in supporting their efforts half a world away, "that have no other purpose than the conversion and civilization of the natives, and that can yield no profit unless God be paymaster." He continued, "It is a more praiseworthy purpose than that of other nations who seek nothing but their own cruel and selfish enrichment."

The natives interested La Pérouse particularly as he described the men as clothed now in a breech cloth, the young girls in a cincture and the women wearing cloth shirts with sleeves, while the children of both sexes were naked. He observed natives in stocks and in chains as well as under the lash for punishment. But he found their religion "nebulous and unexacting" with "all their ancient customs which are not superstitious or degrading being preserved and all amusements being encouraged." He observed that the men hunted and fished, retaining their skill at harpooning otters and salmon." Though covetous, the natives appeared to him to be friendly and hospitable but one facet of their character disturbed him he was understandably "astounded" at the unconcern with which the fathers traded their children for objects that they desired. We would like to know more about this but no further details were given.

La Pérouse, for all his enthusiasm for the land and the support being given to the missionary enterprise by the Spanish government, was not blind to the difficulties with which the missionaries in California were faced, commenting, "The enthusiasm of religion, with the reward that it promises, can alone compensate for the sacrifice, the disgust, the fatigue and the danger which the missionary life entails." And another member of the expedition wrote, "The zeal for the propagation of the faith has already resulted in several missions; but the country is of so little importance that even privateers would hardly think it worth their while to disturb the pious exercises of the ecclesiastics."

Anxious to leave a small contribution for the life at Mission San Carlos Borromeo, the French explorer presented the padres with seed potatoes and fruit tree sprouts from Chili and many containers of vegetable seeds brought with him from France. A 'semi-portable' flour mill was also left by the Frenchmen but there is no proof that it was ever used, the native women preferring their traditional mortar and pestle for the milling of their seeds. Today in the cemetery at the side of the mission church are two millstones which show no signs of wear. Are these unused stones left from the mill which was a gift of La Pérouse?

This French expedition which has left for us so much information about the Carmel mission was destined for a tragic end. After moving up the coast of North America they proceeded across the ocean to the Russian settlements in Siberia. From there they sent copies of their reports and sketches overland to France, and continued south to Australia. There, in Botany Bay, La Pérouse was met by an English ship in February 1788 and that was the last that was heard of his expedition. Thirty-eight years later evidence of the wrecking of the two expedition ships was found on the reefs of the New Hebrides islands to the northeast.

While the ships of the French expedition were in the Monterey harbor there were also anchored there two Spanish supply ships, the *Princessa* and the *Favorita*. The former had brought Don Vicente Vasadne, who arrived with a royal sanction to attempt to interest the padres in a scheme for the hunting of the sea otters for export of their furs. His plan was to exchange the pelts in Canton, where the fur was in great demand, for Chinese quicksilver. The fur of the sea otter, which has 650,000 hairs per square inch and is twice as thick as that of the seal, was highly valued for capes, belts and borders of robes by the wealthy Chinese nobles.

Both Governor Fages and Fr. Lasuén were enthusiastic about this opportunity to participate in such lucrative trade and the word went out from Carmel that the missions should assist in the project. On the instructions of the padres the neophytes throughout California began to kill the sea otters and gather the pelts for which they were given desired goods in exchange. The pelts were then sold to Vasadne for between two and ten pesos each for the benefit of the mission funds. In three months 1,060 sea otter skins were loaded on the *Princessa,* with San Carlos mission providing the largest number, though skins were gathered from all five of the missions in the northern part of California.

This source of income for the missions was destined, however, to be shortlived, for the gathering of otter pelts was too lucrative a project to be left in the hands of the Friars. In 1788 the regulation of the trade was changed, giving the *Habilitados* (Paymasters) of the Presidios the exclusive right to purchase the pelts from the natives. The *Habilitados* were soon accused of cheating the natives and it was found that payments made in cash were the least desirable means of exchange—in that year only seventy-six skins were provided from Carmel. Two years later the padres were again put in control of the collection of the pelts for a short time in order to correct the abuses of the trade, but at the insistance of the Presidio merchants the new rule was nullified in a few months. After that the missionaries were no longer involved in the trade which was in time to bring the species to near extinction.

The coastline of California and the borders of the offshore islands were said to have been "covered like a thick black fringe" in mission times by this unique marine mammal, which was to be found only along the shores of the Pacific Ocean from the coast of Japan through the Kurile and Aleutian islands, then down the west coast of the American Continent from Alaska to Baja California. But between 1741 and 1900,

Photograph of the sea otter exhibit in the Pacific Grove Museum.

when an international agreement for the protection of the species was finally made, as many as a million sea otters were killed for their pelts by Spanish, Russian, English and American fur traders. The Russian American Fur Company, formed by the Russian government, extended its activities from Japan to Alaska and down the coast to Fort Ross (Fort Rus or Russian Fort), about seventy miles north of San Francisco Bay.

The California sea otter (*Enhydra lutris nereis*) was thought to be extinct until a 'raft', as a colony of sea otters is called, of about 120 members was sighted in 1935 off Bixby Cove on the Big Sur shore. These playful creatures which today can be observed near the shore from Monterey Bay to Morro Bay are notable as the only subprimate tool-using mammals. In a pouch made from the folds of skin under its front legs each will keep a double fist-size stone.  As the otter swims on its back this stone will be moved to its chest and used to break the shells of the molluscs held in its paws. The sea otter is the last of the land mammals to become a marine animal but, unlike the whale, dolphin and seal, it has retained the form of a land animal. Though from time to time one may be seen hauling itself ashore, perhaps to sleep a part of the night there, it is a half mile off shore that it mates, bears its young and spends its whole life swimming and floating with its fellows in a 'raft'. Still the young sea otter must be taught to swim, for it is born with no knowledge of the sea. Until the young one is able to swim the mother will often set it on a clump of seaweed to hold it up while she dives for food, then will return to carry the pup on her chest as she floats on her back.

Though the missionaries got out of the fur business in 1790 the expansion of the mission herds and farmlands was already arousing the envy of civilians and civilian authorities in California. Three years earlier the Adjudent Inspector of Presidios had presented a plan for the secularization of the missions and the division of the lands among the mission's neophytes. While the Padre-Presidentes Serra and Lasuén had not always found Fages a cooperative coworker since he had first arrived in Monterey as a lieutenant in Portolá's party in 1770, it is to his credit that, as governor of California, he opposed this plan for the secularization of the missions. He argued that both the spiritual and temporal progress of the natives were due to the zeal of the padres and that these primitive people were better off under mission care. The missions of California were saved through Fages's good offices and their most prosperous years were yet to come.

Yet trouble did develop at this time between the authorities at Mission San Carlos in Carmel and the government officials in Monterey. Lasuén was so concerned with his task of administration of all the missions of California and the establishment of new ones that he was often away from Carmel. The padre who was left in charge in his absence, Fr. Noriega, was evidently a very strict disciplinarian. Governor Fages received accusations that the neophytes at Carmel had been beaten with chains for certain offenses. Denying this, the padre brought the counter charge that the civil authorities were wont to condemn the natives for crimes that they had not committed in order to obtain prisoners as laborers at the Presidio. There was probably some basis for all these accusations for the system did allow for some abuses both at the missions and at the Presidio.

The soldiers at the Presidio were not anxious to turn their hand at anything that they could find prisoners to do, while the padres found that only physical punishment had any effect on the natives under their charge. In theory the baptized natives were at an advantage over the unbaptized, 'gentile' natives because the mission provided food and clothing as well as housing for them. But for these advantages the neophytes were required to stay at the mission except for occasional visits with relatives in the gentile *rancherias*. There was the danger, as the padres saw it, that if the neophytes were allowed to stay away too long among the gentiles they would backslide into paganism. There was also the need for the neophyte labor to produce the food which was freely distributed to all at the mission compound and adjoining neophyte *rancheria.*

In order to preserve the system the rule was established that neophytes who left their mission adobes for any length of time would be hunted down with the help of the soldiers, returned to the mission and punished. Every mission had its whipping post at which runaways and others who had broken the rules were punished. There was probably some excessive use of the lash at the California missions, for stern conditions of life sometimes lead to mental aberration even among those under strict monastic vows. Indeed, it is recorded that more than one missionary of the time became violently insane and had to be sent back to the mother house in Mexico City.

Moreover, the situation must be seen in the light of the attitude of people of that day. During the eighteenth century more than a hundred offenses were punishable by death in Europe and whipping was a normal penalty. The stocks, which were often used in eighteenth-century America, proved to be of little corrective value for the native, who would simply relax as he waited for release. Therefore some form of physical punishment was required to keep order in the community. It must be remembered that the padres were stern ascetics, applying physical punishments to themselves or wearing hair shirts next to their skin 'for the good of their souls'. As they devoutly believed that mortification of the flesh brought the soul a little closer to heaven, all punishment of the natives was sincerely believed to be 'for their own good'.

During this period Lasuén continued his activity in extending the mission chain. In 1787 he founded the Mission La Purísima Concepción (The Immaculate Conception) near the point of land at the head of the Santa Barbara Channel which had been so named by Velasquez. This post, approximately midway between the Missions San Luis Obispo and Santa

Barbara, was the first of the links which Lasuén was to found as he established what came to be called *El Camino Real* (The Royal Highway). Four years later he founded Mission Santa Cruz (Holy Cross) to the north of Carmel and Mission Nuestro Señora de Soledad (Our Lady of Solitude) to the south as stations on *El Camino Real* radiating from the Mission San Carlos. During his seventy-seventh year, between June 1797 and June 1798, he established the five missions of San José de Guadalupe (St. Joseph of Guadalupe, patron saint of California) on the slopes of the Diablo Mountain Range between Santa Clara and San Francisco; San Juan Bautista (St. John the Baptist) between San Carlos and Santa Cruz; San Miguel Arcángel (St. Michael Archangel) between San Luis Obispo and San Antonio de Padua; San Fernando Rey de España (St. Ferdinand King of Spain) between San Gabriel and San Buenaventura; and San Luis Rey de Francia (St. Louis King of France) between San Juan Capistrano and San Diego.*

*El Camino Real* was so called because along it the traveler could safely and conveniently travel the length of California, from San Diego to San Francisco, under what amounted to the protection of the King of Spain. Lasuén had completed this 'Royal Highway' by establishing these additional missions between those founded by Serra so that the journey between one mission and another could be made in a day's ride. Moreover, the traveller along this route knew that the natives in the countryside posed no threat, for most were converted Christians with an established loyalty to the Church. He could also anticipate a warm reception for him each night at a hospitable mission. Nowhere else in America away from the settled east coast was such a safe and convenient highway known for many

---

* Three missions were founded after the death of Lasuén: Santa Inés (St. Agnes) in 1804 between Santa Barbara and La Purísima; San Rafael Arcángel (St. Raphael Archangel) and San Francisco de Solano (St. Francis of Solano) in 1817 and 1823 north of San Francisco.

years to come. The present-day, north-south road in California still carries the name El Camino Real, and is marked by the symbolic bell that reminds one of the mission bells which once rang to welcome the traveler when he came into sight. But the tourist must now depend on fast-food outlets and motels for his accommodations and the California Highway Patrol for his protection.

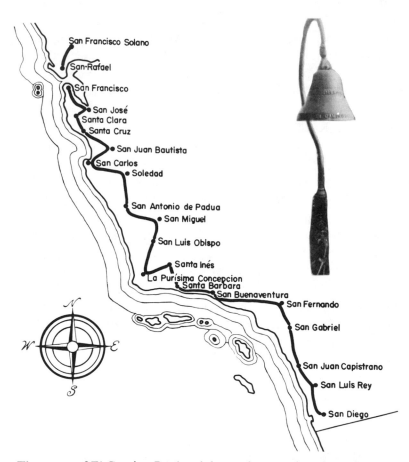

The route of El Camino Real and the modern marker along the route of the highway.

Captain Alessandro Malaspina, an Italian on a world-encircling expedition under the auspices of the Spanish government, was the next foreign visitor to be entertained at Carmel, arriving at San Carlos mission on September 20, 1791. In his reports he noted that throughout California the traveler or the missionary "need not fear crossing all alone and without a guard any forty or fifty leagues inhabited by enemy nations." The arrival of the Spaniards in California, he was surprised to find, had brought to the natives "without the slightest shedding of blood, the end of a thousand local wars that were destroying them, social beginnings and a holy religion, safe and healthy food." About no other conquest in the history of the world could such a statement have been made.

He did express some disappointment with the neophytes who were helping him gather botanical specimens for the scientists who accompanied the expedition. "Lacking the stimulus of private property," he opined, "and the advantages that the most active and hardworking would achieve they only engage in the tasks that they are obliged to perform." In comparison with the natives that he had seen on the northern Pacific Coast he called these "the ugliest and filthiest that can be found."

It must be remembered that these observations were made after a visit of a very few days. Yet the keeping of the neophytes in a permanent *rancheria* at the mission probably did present problems of sanitation. The native's custom was to set up new and fresh *rancherias* as they moved about with the seasons, leaving their collection of refuse (and fleas) behind them. If they were too long in one place they would simply burn their *rucs* and depart to set up a new *rancheria* nearby. With no chance to move from the mission *rancheria* their system of 'natural sanitation' was upset and there was probably less use of the *temescal*, the aboriginal sauna which they used for body cleansing, when they became mission laborers. The visitor who had no chance to observe them in their native state might well think of the natives in their new situation as 'filthy and ugly'.

Malaspina could not understand "the lack of competitive spirit and of the urge to hard labor" which he found among these people. He even resented the abundance of the readily gathered seafood which the environment provided for those native to this land, which led to what he considered "a life of perpetual inaction and uselessness." Though he did not report that the natives were skillful hunters, he commented critically on the fact that "in their *rancherias* they make their meals of seafood that the sea spreads upon the beach in unspeakable abundance, thus saving them the work of fishing and preparing the equipment necessary for it." One wonders what he would have made of the Sandwich Islanders (Hawaiians), who were described by a contemporary of that time as "dusky fisher folk who were plying their business not with the fierce energy of western workers who rise early to wage war with the hours, but with the happy languor of those who have no quarrel with time and know that the whole day is before them, one long free leisure, in which they can easily catch and prepare and enjoy the bounty of the sea." Malaspina's comments reveal as much about the captain himself and the possession-seeking society that he represented as they do about the Carmel natives. Perhaps this may explain why we of modern 'accomplishment-oriented' civilization often have trouble in understanding people of a different orientation.

The drawing made by José Cardero, the artist with the Malaspina expedition, was made from the area seen to the left in the de Vancy sketch of the La Pérouse reception. The porches of the *Xacalon Grande* and the Serra adobe church, the ring of bells and Serra's large cross are on the left of Cardero's sketch, with the *rancheria* of the married neophytes beyond. The building with the three doors in the right background was the priests' quarters. In front of the priests' quarters is the whipping post.

A sketch of the Carmel mission compound made in 1791 by José Cardero, the artist with the Malaspina expedition. (Courtesy of the Downie Collection)

The manner in which adobe buildings were built is illustrated in the foreground of Cardero's sketch. The roof was first raised, held up by tree trunks and covered with tule. Then the walls of adobe bricks were built under the roof, which protected the unbaked bricks from the weather.

From the reports of the Malaspina expedition we receive additional information regarding the marriage customs of the Rumsens. Malaspina found that the men generally had two, three or four wives, a practice which had not been reported elsewhere in comments on the natives. This custom of multiple wives, he opined, led to another practice which was widely followed—the females' use of abortion to preserve both their beauty and the favor of the common husband.

A year after Malaspina's visit, the first English visitor, Captain George Vancouver, arrived at Mission San Carlos Borromeo. He entered Monterey Harbor at the end of November 1792. With his fellow officers he visited the mission on the Carmel River where he reports that he was "handsomely entertained" at dinner in an outdoor bower set up to handle the large party. As a part of the entertainment the neophytes demonstrated their hunting technique. José Cardero's drawing must have been made at such a display for Point Lobos can be seen in the background.

Sketch of Rumsen native made by José Cardero. (Museo Naval, Madrid)

A drawing made by John Sykes, artist with the Vancouver expedition, in 1793. (Courtesy of the Downie Collection)

John Sykes, the artist with Vancouver, also made a sketch of the Carmel mission compound. It differed greatly from Cardero's drawing, done only two years earlier, for by 1793 all the preparations for the great stone church were underway. By the time Vancouver arrived, both the *Xacalon Grande* and the Serra adobe church had been torn down to make room for the stone building which was to occupy the site of Serra's adobe. The small cross in the right center of the sketch locates the site of the adobe church, for it marked the graves of Serra and Crespí which were inside the chancel of that demolished building. When the permanent church was constructed in the same location it was so built that the graves of the two priests were inside the chancel, where they may be seen today.

A "provisional church" was built to serve while the stone church was being constructed. This provisional church can be seen to the left in the Sykes drawing with the large cross erected by Serra in 1771 standing prominently before it and the ring of bells in a temporary location nearby. These bells were to be placed in the tower of the new stone church.

The new kiln which was built to bake the roof tiles for the permanent church is in the left background. The small group to the left of the cross marking the graves must represent a work party gathering stones for the new construction. The native brown sandstone of which the church was to be built was described by Vancouver in his records of the Carmel visit as being "of a very friable nature, scarcely more than indurated clay" which became very hard soon after it was exposed. Mortar and plaster were made from lime from abalone shells which abounded on the *middens* to be found all about the beach. The walls were five feet thick at the base, widening as the inner wall curved inward to support the arch of the ceiling. Though the present ceiling of the church, which is now used as the parish church for Carmel, is made of wood painted to look like stone, the inward arching walls still give this 'curious effect' which is unique in mission construction.

Manuel Estevàn Ruiz, a master mason, had taken charge of the construction of the stone church. He had been brought from Mexico to supervise the construction of a church at the presidio in Monterey. When work there was completed he came to Carmel to build the permanent stone church at Mission San Carlos. Ruiz, who had built the church at San Blas in Baja California and worked on many other churches in Mexico before coming to Monterey, patterned the Carmel and Monterey churches after those he had known in Mexico and so set the 'Spanish style' of the California missions.

This permanent stone church was the seventh place of worship to be used at the Carmel mission. The seven were:

The original brush hut put up by Serra in August 1771, alongside the large cross that he raised while the first buildings were being constructed at the mission site. Here the daily mass and other prayer services were held.

The padre's cell, a room used for worship in the log-sided priests' residence which was completed in December 1771.

The first log church, built of upright logs driven into the ground with a roof of tule in 1773 by Fr. Palóu while Fr. Serra was in Mexico City straightening out the affairs of the California missions.

The *Xacalon Grande* (Large Rough), built in 1778 because Palóu's church was beginning to rot. The foundations of this rough building, which was said to be large enough to hold the whole community at services, were discovered by Harry Downie inside the present school patio. The large cypress tree there stands in the midst of the remains of the foundations.

The Serra adobe church, described by La Pérouse as having the interior walls decorated with paintings in the Italian style. It was built in 1782 on the site of the present church building.

The provisional church, built to one side in 1793 when Serra's adobe was demolished so that the stone church could be built in the same location.

The great stone church, which was started in 1793 and completed in 1797, built by the master mason Manuel Estéván Ruiz and used today as the parish church in Carmel.

When Vancouver visited the Carmel mission there were 876 neophytes housed there. Along with the resident padres, the soldiers who served as guards, and the civilian artisans, this was the largest number of people ever to be in residence there. Vancouver considered the native *rancheria* rather small for over eight hundred neophytes, and in reference to the residents commented that "it was not apparent that Christianization had as yet benefitted the general run of converts but there were individuals who had profitted." He expressed his admiration for Fermín Francesco de Lasuén, the Padre-Residente of all the California missions, who was resident at Carmel, characterizing him as "gentle of manner and placid of countenance, tranquil of mind and a truly lovable character." So impressed was he with this padre that he gave the name 'Point Fermin' to the head of San Diego Bay. And he described the Franciscan friars as well as the other Spanish Californians he met as "generous, friendly, kind and most hospitable to strangers." We trust that the tourists who visit Carmel and its mission today will so describe the Californians they meet.

It is said that one of Vancouver's ships sailed for New South Wales, upon departing the California shores, carrying a ram and three ewes from Carmel. These are believed to have been the parent stock for the great flocks which now cover Australia. Two of his other vessels sailed for the Sandwich Islands, now the Hawaiian Islands, carrying cattle to establish the great herds that would develop there. Vancouver arrived at those islands at about the time that Kamehameha was uniting them under one ruler for the first time.

Lasuén's last years were tempestuous ones for the Carmel Mission. In 1801 there were rumors of a native plot to kill the padres there and to burn the adjoining *rancheria*. Both were surrounded by soldiers from the Monterey Presidio. The "plot" was then discovered to be nothing more than the invention of a disgruntled neophyte, and for the second time a threat to the mission proved to be a false alarm. But during the rest of that year and the next, threats of impending plagues proved to be very real. During those two years as many as 150 of the neophytes were taken by the sickness which was referred to as *dolor de costado*, pain of the side, meaning that the symptoms were like those of pneumonia. Only five Spaniards died of the malady, suggesting that this was the beginning of the sort of diseases which were to wipe out many of the Rumsen natives by the early twentieth century.

In his later years Lasuén completed the cataloguing of the library collection which Fr. Serra had begun. There were about four hundred bound volumes in the library at that time, each of which he marked with a white label bearing the number of the book and the number of the case which held it. The reconstructed library room was returned to its original use and appearance in 1950 by Harry Downie, warden of the mission, who set out to find as many of the original volumes as possible. Identifying them by Lausén's original labels, he found volumes in churches and private collections all over California and has been able to reassemble about two-thirds of those in the original colleciton. Only two volumes bear an inscription in Serra's own hand but it is known that many more were collected in his time. Today the reassembled books are in the reconstructed library room, furnished as it was in Lasuén's

The reconstruction of the Carmel mission library, looking today as it did in 1800, with original volumes collected by Frs. Serra and Lasuén.

day. There is also a modern library of more than three hundred volumes and other documents bearing on the history of the San Carlos Basilica. This collection, known as the Harry Downie Library, has been assembled by Mr. Downie during his almost fifty years as warden at the mission. It is available for the use of serious history students and other qualified persons.

Fermín Francisco de Lasuén, who contributed so much to the development of the original library, had served as Padre-Presidente of the California missions four years longer than had Serra. When he died in 1803 at the age of eighty-three he had completed eighteen years in that position. During this time *El Camino Real* was completed with the nine missions which he had founded, and the crude wooden mission churches were replaced throughout California by the fine stone structures that have come to characterize California mission architecture—plastered walls, prominent towers in the Spanish style, and red tile roofs. It might be said that the beautiful mission structures throughout the state, many now rebuilt in the form that they were in in Lasuén's day, are a memorial to that remarkable padre. It is right that Fr. Lasuén, who completed the task that Fr. Serra had begun, should be buried beside the founder of the California missions in the sanctuary of the Mission San Carlos Borremeo.*

Father Estev009Tápis, who was in charge of the Santa Barbara Mission at the time of Lasuén's death, was elected Padre-Presidente in 1803. He remained at Santa Barbara for a few years, then moved up to Carmel, again making San Carlos Borromeo the center of mission activity in California. In 1806 the mission's buildings were augmented with a set of fifty-two

---

*Julian Lopez, a young Franciscan friar who died at the mission in 1797, was buried in the chancel of the church beside his brother Franciscans. Outside the altar rail were interred the bodies of José Antonio Romeau, Gobernador of California, in 1792, and Hermenegildo Sal, Commandante of the Monterey Presidio, in 1800.

little houses to replace the neophyte *rancheria*. And in the next year Fr. Juan Amorós, who was in charge of San Carlos while Fr. Tapís was away on general mission business, added another thirty-seven. For the first time the neophytes attached to the Carmel mission were moved out of their native *rucs* into permanent housing of the sort enjoyed by the Europeans. But this was to prove to be a mistake for the natives had been much healthier as well as happier in the dwellings which they had constructed for themselves.

A drawing made by William Smythe in 1826 shows the Mission San Carlos Borromeo at the height of its development. The houses built for the neophytes are to the right of the

A sketch of the completed Carmel mission, made in 1826 by William Smythe, the artist with the expedition of Frederick William Beechey. (Courtesy of the Downie Collection)

stone church, beyond the road which led from Monterey, an area now occupied by homes of modern Carmelites. Beyond the mission church and the houses for natives are Point Lobos and the open ocean in the Carmel River Bay. In front of the church, just to the left of the entrance doors, are the padres' quarters, and reaching out from these is the row of workshops. The padres' quarters have been reconstructed in their original form and today contain the rooms as they were then—the dining room, common room, kitchen, Serra's cell, and the library, along with the museum which holds a sarcophagus dedicated to the memory of Serra and many of the original vestments and altar pieces. The quarters for the present parish priests have been built on the foundation of the workshops, along with a very beautiful small chapel used for daily mass. A portion of the chapel's outer wall is the one part of the original eighteenth century wall that remained when reconstruction was started and was left unplastered to show the original construction.

The workshops formed one side of the square compound which was surrounded by the mission buildings. In this compound Harry Downie found the remains of the base of the wooden cross raised there by Serra in 1771, with the stones that held the base in place. He has re-erected a cross in the form of the original. It is in the large patio, just outside the museum entrance. On another side of the compound was the *monjerio*, the quarters for the unmarried female neophytes. The hospital and other mission buildings completed the square, where now stand the classrooms of the Junípero Serra School.

The fountain in the middle and the covered walkway around the enclosed space give the mission patio the appearance it had when used by the padres and their neophyte flock at the beginning of the nineteenth century. The many tourists who visit the mission every day may now stand in the midst of the rebuilt patio, looking toward the restored cross of Fr. Serra with the two towers of Fr. Lasuén's stone church beyond.

Letting their imaginations travel back in time to the days of California's founding padres, they must feel some of the magic of the Mission San Carlos Borromeo seen as it was at the height of its prominence.

## Bibliographical Notes

The reports of La Pérouse were published as *Voyage de la Pérouse, Autor du Monde, redige par M. L. A. Milet-Mureau* in four volumes with a volume of maps (Paris, 1797). A new English version, somewhat condensed, has recently been published by the University of Hawaii Press as *Voyages and Adventures of La Perouse* (1969). Malaspina's visit is surveyed in a fine recent volume, *Malaspina in California* by Donald C. Cutter (San Francisco, 1960). It is based on Malaspina's journals. Vancouver's reports were published as *A Voyage of Discovery* in three volumes (London, 1789).

# THREE

# Secularization
# Brings Ruin

t was the very success of the California missions that
led to their destruction. As the great wealth accumulated by
the English monastic houses by the sixteenth century had
encouraged Henry VIII to bring about the dissolution of the
monasteries there, so the prosperity of the California missions
in the early nineteenth century presaged their secularization.
At their height the Franciscan missions in California owned as
many as 232,000 head of cattle, 34,000 horses, and 3,500 mules,
in addition to goats, swine and herds of sheep. The missions
were providing sustenance for the whole of the military and
civilian government personnel from 1810, when all government support ceased in the state, to 1835, when the secularization of the missions was complete. Of course, all property was
held in the names of the native neophytes attached to the
missions, for the padres, serving under their vow of poverty,
could own nothing. The 145 friars who had come to California
between 1769 and 1835 had converted some forty thousand
neophytes and had opened the great expanses of land on the
Pacific Coast to farming and pasturage. It was this land that
was now sought by the governments of Spain and Mexico and
later by the adventurers who flocked to California in the
nineteenth century.

The support for the missions, since their founding, had come not from the Spanish government but from the income from what was known as the 'Pious Fund'. This fund had been built up from gifts of money, estates and factories donated to the Jesuit Order for the support of their missionary work. When that order was suppressed in 1768 the fund went to support other missionary activities, yielding at one time about $50,000 a year.* Then when the Order of Franciscans took over the missions of Baja California from the Jesuits the income from the Pious Fund continued to support these missions. When the Franciscans moved into Alta California under the leadership of Fr. Serra in 1770, the Pious Fund supported the new establishments to the north. In 1810 the fund was seized by the government authorities in Mexico City, and with this move no more supply ships were to be sent north. The California missions were left to support themselves.

By that time the herds of cattle on the mission lands had made it possible for the missions to be independent, supporting themselves by trading hides and tallow with the ships that came to the California ports. On the occasions known as the

---

*The sign "$" represents Spanish *pesos*, from which it was adopted as the sign for the U.S. dollar. It is said that the "$" sign represents the Pillars of Hercules (Gibralter) from the Spanish coat of arms as engraved on the face of the silver *peso*. First coined by Ferdinand and Isabella in 1497, these came to be the basis for the silver coinage of the Spanish empire at the time of the monetary reform of 1772–86. Called by Americans the "Spanish milled dollar," the silver *peso* was the prototype of the U.S. silver dollar which had the same value.

The silver *pesos* had a value of eight *reales* each so they came to be known popularly in the U.S. as "pieces of eight." And since the U.S. coin for the quarter dollar was worth two *reales* it came to be known as "two bits," the half dollar as "four bits," and seventy-five cents as "six bits."

Spanish coins of two, four, six and eight *reales* were found in the ruins of the mission buildings by Harry Downie as he excavated for the rebuilding of the mission in the 1930s. They are to be seen today in the middle of the Guest Dining Room in the restored Padre's Quarters.

*matanza* (slaughter) the cattle chosen to be taken were driven in groups of fifty to a spot near a brook and there slaughtered and stripped of their hides and fat. Then came the 'trying out' of the tallow as it was purified by boiling in great vats sunk into the ground. The hides were stretched out to dry and were then

Native women "trying out" the tallow from the mission herds. (Mission Trails Association)

stored until the next trading ship arrived. The small portion of the meat that was to be preserved was cured in the sun for local use and for sale to the ship suppliers. An attempt was made at one time to salt the meat and store it in barrels for later sale and shipment in order to make some use of the carcasses that were otherwise left to rot. But the enterprise was not successful so great collections of carrion flesh continued to be left for the scavenger birds.

In 1813 the second threat of secularization was felt by the missions. In that year, an act passed in the Spanish *Cortes* (legislative assembly), all missions in the Americas which were over ten years old were to be immediately handed over to the secular authorities. One-half of the mission lands were to be divided among the native neophytes and the other half sold to help pay Spain's national debt. Fortunately for the padres the bishops in Mexico did not have enough secular priests to take the place of the friars, so the act was not implemented in California. As Governor Fages had resisted the plan of the Adjudant Inspector of Presidios for the secularization of the missions in 1793, so now again the dissolution of the Franciscan missionary enterprise in California was avoided.

A year later a part of the fabric of the Carmel mission was to be taken away. The stone vault over much of the nave was seen to be cracked. For safety the vaulted ceiling was taken down, except over the chancel from the last arch to the altar wall. It has been supposed that the crack was a result of the shaking caused by the devastating California earthquake of 1812. At that time forty worshippers were crushed when the stone church at the San Gabriel mission crumbled, and mission buildings were destroyed at Santa Barbara, Santa Inés, and La Purisima Concepción. Perhaps it could better be viewed as an omen of the gradual destruction of the buildings at the Mission San Carlos Borromeo which was to come within a few years. The vaulting over the chancel lasted for another forty years, falling in 1851.

Annual reports were required from the California missions by the Mexican government after 1795 for the information of the Spanish king. The annual report of the Carmel mission, called "Mission San Carlos of Monterey," dated February 3, 1814, is given in full in English translation in Fr. Zephyrin Engelhardt's book on Mission San Carlos.* This report is of particular interest because of the information regarding the

---

*Fr. Zephyrin Engelhardt, *Mission San Carlos Borromeo (Carmelo) The Father of the Missions*, pp. 120-134.

natives and their language that was included therein by Fr. Juan Amorós, who was in charge of the mission that year. According to that report the seven tribes or subtribes, members of which lived at the mission that year, were the Esselen, Egeac, Rumsen, Sargent Ruc, Sarconeños, Guachirron and Calenda Ruc. The two main groups were the Rumsen of Carmel Valley and the Esselen of the Monterey area.

There was included in that report a brief comment on the differing dialects of the Rumsen and Esselen tribes. The transliteration of the native words was given for the statement which in English would be: "Men who are good bowmen are esteemed and well liked." To the padres the statement in the two native tongues sounded thus: In the Rumsen dialect, "Maxina Muguianc jurrigning igest oyh laguan eje uti maigin" and in the Esselen dialect, "Eg enoch lalucuimos talogpami ege salegua lottos, takeyapami lasalachis." (The capitalization and punctuation follow that of the report.) Nothing could show more plainly how far apart these neighboring tribes kept themselves before the missionaries arrived to convert them to a common faith than this great difference in their spoken tongues.

The year after this report was made orders came through from Mexico that the missions would be responsible for the support of the presidio personnel who were there supposedly to protect them. Padre-Prefect (as the director of the California missions was then known) Vicente Francisco Sarría gave the order to those in charge of each mission, and from that time California was on its own with a self-supporting economy dependent upon the missions. This support was possible, of course, only through the trade with the ships that called to collect the tallow and hides. Though the ports were by law closed to all but Spanish ships, no attempt was made to enforce this rule and there were actually British, French, Russian and American vessels in one California port or another at any time. It is reported that one Yankee ship, the *Traveller*, sold $700

worth of goods to the soldiers and their families at the
Monterey Presidio in 1817, as well as a supply of altar linens
and candles and cloth for native garb to the missionaries at
Carmel.

Not all visiting ships brought welcome cargoes, however. In
November of 1818 the pirate Hippolyte Bouchard brought his
two ships, the *Chica* and the *Negra* into Monterey Harbor and
opened fire on the fort above the town. Though the arrival of

A print taken from the portrait of Hippolyte Bouchard painted in
Buenos Aires. (Courtesy of Colton Hall collection)

the freebooter from Buenos Aires had been expected and Governor Pablo Vicente de Solá had brought in *vaqueros*\* (cattlemen) from the mission ranges to augment the force at Monterey, the battle was a brief one. When Bouchard landed men from small boats at Point Pinos to attack the fort from the land side, the defenders fled to the presidio compound which was in the middle of the town. And when Bouchard's guns were turned on the presidio, the soldiers fled inland, accompanied by all the residents of Monterey. The civilians took refuge in the Soledad mission while the troops gathered at the Rancho del Rey near the present town of Salinas with Father de Sarría as their chaplain. The only Monterey casualty was a man named Monila who was captured. He was taken, it is said, because he was too drunk to flee with the others. Five of the raiders were killed and three captured. The pirate offered to spare the town if the captured members of the crew were released. When this offer was rejected Bouchard proceeded to destroy the presidio, its garden and orchard, and all the homes of the surrounding village. A silver spoon which was recovered by a member of the Munras family from the ruins of the burned presidio is to be seen today in the Munras Museum at the Carmel mission.

Fr. Amorós and the other padres, civilians, and neophytes of the Carmel mission fled up the Carmel River, but Bouchard's crew failed to discover the mission on the bank of the river. Evidently the hills between Monterey and Carmel, which made hard pulling for teams of horses for many years and were later a problem for the highway builders, proved in this case to be the salvation of the Carmel mission. It was reported that the freebooter seized goods valued at $5,000 in Monterey before he withdrew five days after arriving, but the mission with its treasures of silver crosses, candlesticks and other valuable

---

\*In U.S. slang the Spanish *vaquero* became the cowboy "buckaroo" as the Spanish *le reata* (the rope) became our "lariat."

possessions which had been collected over almost half a century was left inviolate.

A year later, however, the arrival of two Spanish ships, the *San Carlos* and the *La Reina de los Angeles*, brought to the Carmel mission trouble which it had been spared previously. Those ships brought a hundred infantrymen for the Monterey Presidio who were to prove to be such troublemakers that Governor de Solá attempted to move them to the mission in order to get them out of the Monterey village. These untrained men, taken from jails or picked up by pressgangs in New Galacia, came to be known as *cholos*, the term for half-breeds or half-civilized men. These short, dark-skinned men of mixed race were resented by the Californians on whom they were foisted and served to increase the antipathy that was growing between any newcomers from Mexico and the *paisanos*, the "*hijos del país*" (sons of the land), as the Californians were beginning to be called.

Knowing that these *cholos* could do nothing but cause trouble, Fr. Sarría decided to refuse to accept them at the mission. But since the neophyte population at Carmel had decreased from the high of 878 in 1795 to 397 in 1819, he could not claim that there was a lack of space for housing them at the mission. Therefore thirty of them were sent to Carmel where they were put in an empty warehouse with one officer to control them. There was immediate conflict as the *cholos* began to force into the *rucs* of the native *rancheria* adjacent to the mission to start fights with the men and attempt to seduce the women. Within two weeks Sarría reported to the Governor that soldiers had seized a native woman, taking her from her *ruc*. But the soldier went unpunished, as far as the record goes.

We do have a report of the punishment ordered by the Governor for an unmarried native woman who was delivered of a child. The instructions issued by Governor de Solá were: "Shave her head with a razor and on the first Feastday let her be seated in a chair in the middle of the Plaza with her head uncovered so that the entire public may see her for two hours before and after Mass." In the East it was a 'scarlet letter', in California a shaven head exhibited for all to see, but in both cases it was the woman who was made to suffer.

The missions of California had been affected very little by the conquest of Spain by Napoleon in 1807, the rule of his brother Joseph until Ferdinand VII was restored by Wellington in 1814, and the uprisings that had occurred in Mexico during those years. Even the short-lived independence movement under José María Morelos from 1813 to 1815 did not touch this distant province. But when an independent Mexico finally came under the leadership of Agustin de Iturbide in 1822, with his short term as King Iturbide I, change was bound to be felt. Governor de Solá resigned his office to become a delegate from California to the Mexican Congress, and the first Legislative Assembly of California met in Monterey under the leadership of the pro-tem Governor, Captain Luis Antonio Argüello.

Fr. Sarría refused to take the oath of loyalty to the new Mexican government, believing that he was still bound by his oath to the Spanish monarch. When the news reached Mexico City that the Padre-Prefect had refused to take the required oath, an order was despatched that Sarría be arrested and deported to Mexico. The new California Governor, José María Echeandia, arrived in February, 1825, but chose to remain in San Diego rather than going to the Provincial Capital of Monterey. He ordered the 'house arrest' of Sarría instead of deporting him to Mexico, explaining to the authorities there, "the departure of the Padre-Prefect and of the many Religious who would follow him, in my judgment would occasion much disquietude in the territory . . . the lack of missionaries would cause disorder in the establishments of the neophytes who are in their charge and which they have been able to preserve in the same state. I have, therefore, not urged the quick departure of Fr. Sarría until the time when a sufficient number of missionaries might relieve those who by reason of the law must leave the Republic." Echeandia was well advised in his decision, for although Sarría left the other Franciscans in California free to make their own decisions in the matter of the oath, twenty of them similarly refused to swear allegiance to the Mexican Constitution. It is hard to imagine the situation if all these had been deported at once.

The Padre-Prefect remained at the Carmel mission, from which he continued to direct the Franciscan missionaries in California but without the possibility of carrying out his periodical canonical visitations. Though Sarría was sixty-two years old, he offered to leave California for the Sandwich Islands (the present Hawaiian Islands) in order to preach to the Kanakas there. His request was refused because the Pacific

The Carmel mission as it appeared early in the nineteenth century. (Courtesy of the Downie Collection)

Islands were considered to be too close to California. Governor Echeandia was ordered to provide Sarría with a European passport and to send him from California on the first available ship, but the Governor continued to procrastinate and Sarría remained at Carmel under house arrest.

On July 25, 1826, the Governor issued a proclamation from his headquarters in San Diego which provided that any married native who had been a Christian for fifteen years and could prove his ability to support himself was free to leave the mission. At San Diego, of the fifty-five men who had the qualifications to depart the mission, only two chose to do so at once. But within a year the neophytes began to scatter. In the next year twenty-three neophytes severed their connection with the Carmel mission. The natives who had been trained as "masons, carpenters, plasterers, soap-makers, tanners, shoe-makers, blacksmiths, millers, bakers, cooks, brick-makers, carters and cart-makers, weavers and spinners, saddlers, agriculturists and herdsmen" were in great demand by the *paisanos* throughout California.* Within two years 233 natives had left the Mission San Carlos and since the mission was required to supply the presidio force with food, there were hardly enough neophytes remaining to tend the cattle and work the fields. The buildings were beginning to fall into disrepair for lack of workers to repair them.

It has been estimated that in the first years of the nineteenth century the missions of California furnished the presidios with the equivalent of $18,000 worth of supplies each year. For this support of the presidios the missionaries were issued with notes on the government which were proving to be worthless. By 1820 the outstanding drafts owed to the missions amounted to approximately $400,000. It became evident that only by the

---

*Native occupations listed in a special report of B. D. Wilson for the U.S. Department of the Interior in 1853, quoted by Helen Hunt Jackson in *Glimpses of California*, p. 71.

seizure of the mission property and assets under the guise of secularization could the Mexican government avoid the payment of its obligations. In effect this was to prove to be a form of what has come lately to be called "nationalization" as nations have seized the assets of independent ventures.

Governor Echeandia came up to Monterey in January 1831 to make a proclamation on his own authority which decreed the immediate secularization of all the California missions. It is said that Echeandia had conspired with José María, a *paisano*, to take over the mission properties and assets for themselves. But a month after Echeandia's proclamation of secularization a newly appointed Governor, Manuel Victoria, arrived in Monterey and at once suspended the execution of his predecessor's decree. Once again, it seemed, the missions were saved from dissolution. Governor Victoria followed the policy of Echeandia in regard to Fr. Sarría, writing to the authorities in Mexico City to this effect.

Though the California missions were saved from secularization for a time, the Spanish Franciscans were soon to be replaced in the oversight of the missions that they had founded. On January 15, 1833, a new Governor, José Figueroa, sailed from San Blas in Baja California with ten native Mexican Franciscans who were to take over the northern California missions from the Spanish padres. The new arrivals were called *Zacatecans* because they were from the Franciscan Missionary College of Guadalupe in Zacatecas, Mexico, to distinguish them from those known as *Fernandinos*, the Spanish Franciscans who had been sent from the College of San Fernando in Mexico City. The Mexican government had decreed that all Spaniards who would not become Mexican citizens by pledging the oath of loyalty should leave Mexican soil. Most of the Spanish Franciscans chose to leave California and return to Spain. But Fr. Sarría elected to remain with his California converts. It is said that he died of starvation at the altar of Mission Soledad after saying his last mass there in 1838.

A sketch which pictures the reception of the Zacatecan Franciscans by the Fernandino Franciscans at Monterey. (Mission San Carlos Borromeo by Fr. Z. Engelhardt)

The Zacatecan padres who landed at Monterey assumed the direction of all the northern missions from San Carlos at Carmel to San Francisco Solano in Sonoma. Fr. Francisco Garcia Diego, who served as the new Commissary Prefect, went to Mission Santa Clara, while Fr. Rafael Moreno came to Carmel as the Padre-Presidente. In his report to Governor Figueroa in 1833 Fr. Moreno stated, "Your honor knows how very few *Indios* this Mission contains, and half of these are invalids by age or infirmity. Moreover some have run away and others, the majority, will not work even if they are chastised." There was a total of 185 baptized natives, men, women and children, at Mission San Carlos at this time.

It was in that year, 1833, that the Mexican Congress had

definitely ordered the secularization of all the California missions. And on November 3, 1834 the California Assembly followed up by authorizing the confiscation of all the mission properties, requiring that an inventory be made at each mission. At Carmel the mission properties were valued at $46,922 and seven *reales*. Of this the church represented more than $10,000, with the church furnishings and library valued at $10,217 in the inventory signed by Padre José María Reál and the lay commissioner José Joaquin Gomez. The mission church was united with the Monterey parish under a Curacy with a resident priest assigned to Carmel until 1839, to minister to the natives who remained in the area, working their allotments along the river.

It is from this period that we have the first report of the Carmel mission and the Monterey village by a citizen of the United States. Charles Henry Dana had sailed from Boston around the Horn to California on a ship loaded with merchandise to be sold in California and traded for hides. His experi-

Monterey as it must have looked when Dana arrived in the harbor. (Courtesy of the Colton Hall Collection)

ences were reported in *Two Years Before the Mast*, which became an immediate best seller in the United States and was to serve as a guide book for many of those who came to California in the nineteenth century. Arriving in Monterey Harbor in January 1835, he described the settlement that he saw as "decidedly the pleasantest and most civilized place in California."*

Dana's full description of the situation and of life in this California settlement tells us much about the fate of the natives after they were 'freed' from the mission by Governor Echeandia in 1826. It could be said in describing the Monterey of 1795 when the Carmel mission had its greatest neophyte population, "Not a single Native, Christian or Pagan, is found as a servant, much less a slave in the home of any Mexican or Spaniard."† Yet when Dana visited there just nine years after the promulgation of the decree which allowed the natives to separate themselves from the missions, he reported that in the town of Monterey, "Among the Mexicans there is no working class, the Indians being practically serfs, and doing all the work—two or three being attached to the better houses. And the poorest are able to keep one at least for they have only to feed them and to give them a small piece of coarse cloth and a belt for the men—the pure Indian runs about with nothing upon him but a small piece of cloth kept up by a wide leather belt—and a coarse gown, without shoes or stockings, for each woman."

The natives of California were in much the same position as the blacks in the United States, especially in the southern states, with one important difference. As Dana explained it, "Yet the least drop of Spanish blood, if it be only a quadroon

---

*Richard Henry Dana tells of his visit to Monterey and Carmel in chapters XXVI and XXVII of his *Two Years Before the Mast* (1840). All quotations given here are from those chapters.

---

†Msgr. James Culleton, *Indians and Pioneers of Old Monterey*, p. 148.

or octoroon, is sufficient to raise one from the position of a serf and entitle him to wear a suit of clothes—boots, hat, cloak, spurs, long knife, all complete though coarse and dirty as they may be—and call himself *Español*, and to hold property if he could get any." While the full blooded natives were kept as a lower class in California, the *mestizas* (half-breeds) came to be numbered among the *gente de razon*, literally 'people of reason', the "accepted people." These were considered to be equal to Spaniards born in Spain and to Mexicans born of Spanish descent in all rights and privileges, as were the wives of mixed marriages. Unlike the black in the southern United States who was considered to be a Negro if there was any touch of African blood in his heritage, the native of California was accepted if he or she had a touch of Spanish blood. For this reason there are many descendants of natives in the families of California and when the fact is known it is a cause for pride.

Dana's visit to the Carmel mission came just before the dissolution of the mission system, so he remembered it as a place of hospitality and good will. He tells of a Sunday jaunt from Monterey: "Toward noon we procured horses, and rode out to the Carmel Mission, which is about a league from the town, where we got something in the way of dinner—beef, eggs, frijoles, tortillas and some middling wine—from the major-domo who, of course, refused to make any charge, as it was the Lord's gift, yet received our present, as a gratuity, with a low bow, a touch of the hat, and 'Dios se lo pague.'" This simple report is notable because it was the last report made of the unaffected mission hospitality before the final secularization of the missions took its toll.

According to the Secularization Act of the California Assembly, one-half of the moveable property of each mission was to be divided among the "emancipated persons," that is, the natives who had been living at the mission, and one-half was to go to the secular administrator to be used for religious purposes. The head of each family was to be given 400 square yards of land to live upon and cultivate. As the 'freeing' of the natives had left them in a state of near slavery, so this 'apportionment' of the mission assets and lands was to leave them, within a few years, landless and in a state of abject poverty.

Though in theory all the lands belonged to the missions, before the end of the eighteenth century some land grants of mission lands were being made to ex-soldiers and others of the community who had influence with the Governor. In 1794 Governor Borica had granted what was called an "occupancy permit" to the Rancho Buenavista in the Salinas Valley to two who had been prominent in the settling of California, Joaquín Ysidro Castro, who had come with his wife and family as colonists in the Anza trek, and his son-in-law, José María Soberanes, who had been a member of the guard stationed at the Carmel mission. It had been understood that these settlers were there on the sufferance of the missionaries and that they should vacate when the mission demanded the land back. But when such a demand was made to Borica's successor in 1802, the claim was rejected and the residents of the Rancho given the grant outright. This new Governor, José Joaquín de Arillaga, was the one who began the widespread granting of ranching concession along the Salinas River and in the Monterey area.

With the coming of Governor José Figueroa in 1833 and the activating of the Secularization Act, much land up the Carmel Valley and along the coast was granted in large tracts. In 1834 Figueroa granted the 26,581 acre Rancho los Tularcitos (Little Tules) to Rafael Gomez and the 8,949 acre Rancho el Sur (the South) to Juan Bautista Alvarado. Before his death in September of 1835 he had made grants to Catalina de Munrás of the 8,814 acre Rancho San Franciscito (Little St. Francis) and to Teodoro Gonzales of the 8,814 acre Rancho San Jose y Sur Chiquito (St. Joseph and Little South) which ran from the San

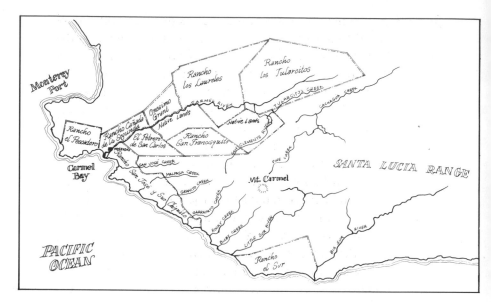

A map showing the original land division in the Carmel Valley and along the coast. (Prepared by Joe Pierre)

Jose Creek to the Little Sur River.

Juan Bautista Alvarado, the first native-born *paisano* to be appointed Governor of California, bestowed twenty-eight land grants during his term in office, 1836–42. His first grant in the area was the 4,426 acre Rancho el Pescadero (the Fisherman) to Fabian Barreto. By the end of the century both the young settlement of Pacific Grove and the hoped-for subdivision of the village of Carmel-by-the-Sea were to come from this Rancho. Among his other grants were the 4,306 acre El Potrero de San Carlos (The Pasture of San Carlos) to Joaquin Gutiérrez in 1837, the 4,367 acre Rancho Cañada de la Segunda (the Second Canyon) to Lazero Soto in 1839, and the 6,624 acre Rancho los Laureles (the Laurels) to José Manuel Boronda.

Though a two-story adobe had been built by Rafael Gomez on Rancho los Tularcitos, the building had remained vacant after Gomez died in an accident with his horse in the grain field. There were to be no permanent resident owners on the ranches of the Carmel Valley until José Boronda, the son of a retired corporal in the Mexican army, moved his family to the Rancho los Laureles in 1840. The repaired building that had formerly housed a native family of mission cattlemen consisted of three rooms with adobe walls, a dirt floor and a tule roof.

The Boronda adobe on the Rancho los Laureles in the Carmel Valley. (Courtesy of the Mayo Hayes O'Donnell Library Collection)

The original Boronda adobe, somewhat altered, is still to be seen in the heart of the valley.

As the family followed the cart tracks from Monterey, past the crumbling mission buildings, they could see the simple dwellings of the natives who were working their allotments of the mission lands along the Carmel River. Their close neighbor was to be a native family consisting of the patriarch Juan Onesimo, his daughter Loretta, her husband Domingo Peralta and their two children. Onesimo, who as a boy had worked on the mission church, had learned to play the violin at the mission and had accompanied the church services on the instrument, which he still treasured. Loretta and Domingo Peralta were favorites at the mission before secularization so that the family received the one sizable tract granted to a native family. They raised corn, tomatoes and onions, which they sold in Monterey, and they were saving to start a herd on their land.

The civil administrator, Antonio Romero, who resented the ownership of such an extent of land by a native family, continually threatened the Peraltas with expulsion, but they had a good friend in Doña Juana Boronda. Doña Boronda encouraged her husband to support the Peraltas before the Governor and is said to have sent gifts of her golden Spanish cheese which was the forerunner of the now famous Monterey Jack cheese. One day the dead body of Domingo Peralta was found on his property and the fate of Onesimo and his family appeared to be sealed. But a previous act of kindness on the part of the Peraltas was to serve to preserve the land for Loretta and her heirs.

In 1837 a British seaman, James Meadows, who had jumped ship at Monterey, was hidden by the Peraltas until his ship sailed. He found work as a *vaquero* at the Rancho el Sur and his friendship with the Peraltas continued. Later he was arrested in Monterey with forty-five other foreigners (mainly ship deserters) and shipped off to prison in Tepic, Mexico.

Clemency was arranged by the British Consul in Mexico and Meadows returned to Monterey in 1841. A year later he married the widow Loretta Peralta and defended her claim to the land. From that time the land was known as the Meadows Grant and James Meadows became a leader in the developing Carmel Valley community. He donated the land and built and furnished the building for the Carmelo School, the first school in the Carmel area.

The Carmelo School building built by James Meadows in the Carmel Valley, with a group of students gathered around their teacher. (Courtesy of the Mayo Hayes O'Donnell Library Collection)

Another daughter of Juan Onesimo, Anselma, married William Brainard Post, who was destined to become a large landowner and a prominent leader in the Monterey community. They were married in 1848, the year that Post arrived in Monterey, and after the Homestead Act of 1862 William and Anselma Post homesteaded extensive acreage south of the

Rancho el Sur. Thus some members of the Onesimo family, like some other natives of the Carmel area, became *gente de razon* by marriage or birth, but they were the fortunate few.

Isabella Meadows, the granddaughter of Juan Onesimo, is said to have provided material for Anne Fisher's novel, *Cathedral in the Sun*, as she related stories about the Carmel mission in its heyday which had been told to her mother by her grandfather. Though a *gente de razon*, she retained pride in her native heritage throughout her life. In 1925, at the age of eighty-nine, she was brought to Washington, D. C., by members of the Smithsonian Institute in order that she could provide a record of the language of the Costanoans, of which the Carmel Rumsens were a sub-tribe. As the last living person to know the speech of her people, she left a valuable record.

When the Borondas moved into the valley, the priest from Monterey was still coming over to Carmel to hold occasional services in the mission church, mainly for the local natives. We have a description of the mission church as it was at that time, left to us by Dr. R. T. Maxwell, who was the assistant surgeon on the frigate *United States* commanded by Commodore Thomas A. P. Catesby Jones. On October 19, 1842 Commodore Jones sailed into the Monterey Harbor, demanding and receiving the surrender of the town in the belief that the United States was already at war with Mexico. When he found that this was not the case he lowered the stars and stripes and sailed down to Los Angeles to apologize to Governor Micheltorena, who had his headquarters there.

Dr. Maxwell remained in Monterey until the following January and left this description of the Carmel church building: "When I was at the Carmel Mission back of Monterey the church was in tolerable repair. There were a number of curious paintings there, and among them one of the landing of Vancouver, a picture about seven feet by eleven, painted chiefly with chrome earth found here, and probably done by one of the ship's painters from his vessel. They presented it to this church. There were twenty-one paintings about eight by twelve, representing Heaven and Hell. Hell was represented by the old mythological characters, while Heaven was represented as a ballroom, with angels and other figures dancing and playing the guitar and tambourine. These were used to convert the Indians. There were some smaller paintings, some of them really beautiful, one of them representing St. John. I, seeing that everything was going to ruin, went to Father Real, and asked him if I could purchase any of the paintings. He said that he could not sell anything belonging to the church but he could not tell whether there were six or sixty pictures; in other words, he was telling me to go and help myself, and not to let him know it. I did not like to do that, however, as an officer of the

A sketch of the Carmel mission made in 1847 by W. R. Hutton. (Courtesy of the Huntington Library Collection)

squadron. What became of these pictures I do not know."* The pictures from the mission church were soon to be scattered as were most of the natives who came to worship there.

Along the road which leads into the Carmel Valley today can still be seen the stump of the tree that was called Descánso

The stump of the Descanso tree, a native resting place, as it is seen today beside the Carmel Valley road. (Photograph by Marguerite Temple)

(resting place) and is symbolic of the fate of the Rumsen natives of the valley. During the period in which the native tracts were still being worked along the river, when a native died the body was brought to the mission for burial, carried by the relatives and friends. The trip was broken for a rest under a tree that grew above a free-flowing spring by the side of the trail. As the burial party rested it was the custom for a small

*Dr. R. T. Maxwell's account of his visit to Monterey and Carmel, dictated several years after his visit to these parts, was finally published in 1955 as *Visit to Monterey, 1842*, J. H. Kemble, ed. This quotation is taken from that work, which is available in the Bancroft Library of the University of California at Berkeley.

cross to be cut into the bark of the tree to mark the occasion. In time the trunk of the large tree was well covered with small crosses. When the road was first paved for automobiles, a large limb over the road was cut off. Then, when the road was widened to four lanes, the remains of the tree, still bearing the crosses, were moved aside and a pull-out area made so travelers could stop to look at the last sign of those who had first inhabited this land. Vandals soon stripped the stump of its crosses but a metal plate was then imbedded in it to explain the history of the tree. Now some 'souvenir hunter', to give so destructive a character the kindest possible appellation, has dug the metal plate out and taken it away. The broken and ravaged tree stump is an appropriate reminder of what has happened to the natives of the Carmel Valley.

The end of the first phase of the life of the Carmel mission might be dated from the time of Governor Manuel Micheltorena, the last California Governor to be sent from Mexico,

A nineteenth century photograph of the Carmel mission in ruins. (Courtesy of the Downie Collection)

who decreed in 1844 that all mission lands should be sold and the money used for the defensive forces of Mexico. Micheltorena was ousted by an uprising of the *Californios* and Pio Pico, a *paisano*, was put in office, but the situation was not improved. Pico put an act through the California Assembly requiring that the disposal of the remaining mission lands be carried out. With the looming threat of war with the United States, the dates of January 2, 3, and 4 of 1846 were set for the auctioning of the Carmel mission. There is no record of any purchase made at the auction of the restricted land area still left to the mission. Squatters moved in to claim the right of possession.

The remaining mission buildings were sold by the government to William Garner of Monterey and subsequently many of the homes and business buildings in Monterey were constructed of timbers and roof tiles taken from the mission. Some of these buildings still stand there.

Services continued to be held periodically in the old mission church, and always on San Carlos Day. These were moved, of necessity, to the sacristy next to the church building because of the threat that the tileless roof of the nave might collapse. On November 4, 1852, San Carlos Day, after mass had been celebrated in the sacristy, the roof did cave in, leaving only the walls of the church standing.

On October 19, 1859 President James Buchanan signed a patent which confirmed the return of the California mission properties to the church. But it appeared that this had come too late for Mission San Carlos Borromeo. The ruined mission buildings were visited in 1861 by a member of a geological survey party, William H. Brewer, who wrote: "It is now a complete ruin, entirely desolate.... Hundreds (literally) of squirrels scampered around in their holes in the old walls ... about half had fallen in ... the paintings and inscriptions on the walls were mostly obliterated. Cattle had free access to all parts; the broken font, finely carved in stone, lay in a corner;

A photograph of the interior of the ruined church of San Carlos Mission after the roof had fallen in. (Courtesy of the Hathaway Collection)

broken columns were strewn around where the altar was; and a large owl flew frightened from its nest over the high altar."*

Yet the Carmel mission was not to die for it was now again in the control of the church and in the charge of the priest at Monterey. Like a phoenix arising from its ashes, this, the first center of missionary activity in California was again to take its place as one of the gems of the rebuilt California mission chain. Before the end of the nineteenth century it was to have a new life and to be the attraction which would bring to life a whole new community at Carmel-by-the-Sea.

---

*Wm. H. Brewer wrote letters to his brother regarding his experiences with the geological survey party in California. These were collected and published as *Up and Down California*, F. P. Farquhar, ed. (1930). His description of the Carmel mission is from this work.

## Bibliographical Note

Useful recent works on the history of the Carmel mission and its surroundings include *Indians and Pioneers of Old Monterey* by Msgr. James Culleton (1950), *Mission to Paradise* by Kenneth M. King, F.I.A.L. (1956/75) and *Mission San Carlos Borromeo, the Father of Missions* by Fr. Zephyrin Engelhardt, O.F.M. (1973). A valuable survey of the history of the whole area is to be found in *Monterey County: The Dramatic Story of Its Past* by Augusta Fink (1972/78).

# FOUR

# The Rebirth
# of the
# Carmel Mission

he ruins of the Carmel mission remained derelict
and forgotten for many years, in the condition described by the
survey party of 1861. Only the wandering cattle came inside the
ruins to graze within the still standing walls, while the squirrels
and owls continued to build their nests among the stones of the
building. One who later was to become world famous for his
writing had an experience with a mission owl which he was not
soon to forget.

Robert Louis Stevenson was enjoying a tryst with his
*inamorata*, Mrs. Fanny Osbourne, among the ruins on a
moonlit night in 1879 when a horrifying scream burst out
overhead. Thinking of the many ghost stories told about the
old mission, the two fled in great fright. It was only when they
had reached the crest of the hill by the mission grounds that
they realized that the cry had come from an owl in the tower
and not from a hidden banshee.

Stevenson had crossed the Atlantic Ocean and the great
American continent to follow a married woman with whom he
had fallen in love when both were visiting in France. Fanny
Osbourne, who was soon to divorce her husband and marry

Stevenson, was living with her sister in the old Spanish-Mexican village of Monterey. There Stevenson came and stayed for some months before the final arrangements were made for his union with Fanny.*

The young writer left us his comments on the Carmel mission as he had found it: "The mission church is roofless and ruinous; sea breezes and sea fogs and the alteration of the rain and the sunshine daily widening the breaches and casting the crockets from the wall. As an antiquity in this new land, a quaint specimen of missionary architecture and a memorial for good deeds, it had a triple claim to preservation from all thinking people; but neglect and abuse have been its portion. There is no sign of American interference save where a headboard has been torn from a grave to be a mark for pistol bullets."†

His thoughts also turned to the fate of the natives whom the mission had been established to serve: "In a comparison between what was and what is California," he wrote, "the praisers of time past will fix upon the Indians of Carmello. The *day of the Jesuits has gone by,*‡ the day of the Yankee has succeeded and there is no one left to care for the converted savage. . . . Their lands, I was told, are being yearly encroached upon by the neighboring American proprietor, and with that exception no man troubles his head of the Indians of Carmel.

---

*The house in which Stevenson stayed is now a part of the tourist attractions in Monterey, and a preparatory school in Pebble Beach has been given the name of the famous author.

---

†Robert Louis Stevenson wrote of Monterey and Carmel in the section titled "Monterey" in his work, *Across the Plains* (1892). All quotations given here are from that section of his work.

---

‡In writing about the long neglected missions of California Stevenson made the natural mistake of assuming that they had been established by Jesuits, the most notable missionary order of the eighteenth and nineteenth centuries, rather than by the members of the Franciscan Order.

The Carmel mission as it appeared when visited by Robert Louis Stevenson and Helen Hunt Jackson at the end of the nineteenth century. (Courtesy of the Downie Collection)

... And it made a man's heart sorry for the good fathers of yore, who had taught them to dig and to reap, to read and to sing, who had given them European mass books which they still preserve and study in their cottages, and who had now passed from all authority and influence in that land—to be succeeded by greedy land thieves and sacrilegious pistol-shots."

From Stevenson's recollections we have a picture of the annual service of worship that had been held at the Carmel mission since the property had been returned to the church some twenty years earlier: "Only one day in the year, the day before our Guy Faux,* the *padre* drives over the hill from Monterey; the little sacristy, which is the only covered portion of the church, is filled with seats decorated for the service; the Indians troop together, their bright dresses contrasting with

---

*Guy Faux Day is kept in England on November 5, the date on which, in 1605, Guy Faux (or Fawkes) was arrested in the vaults under the House of Parliament with thirty-six barrels of gunpowder, with which he planned to blow up the building. On that day it is traditional to light large bonfires and to set off fireworks all around Great Britain.

their dark and melancholy faces; and there, among a crowd of somewhat unsympathetic holiday makers, you may hear God served with perhaps more touching circumstances than in any other temple under heaven. One Indian, stone blind and about eighty years of age, conducts the singing; other Indians compose the choir; yet they have the Gregorian music at their finger ends, and pronounce the Latin so correctly that I could follow the meaning as they sang. The pronunciation was odd and nasal, the singing hurried and staccato. 'In Saecula saeculo-ho-horum,' they went, with a vigorous aspirate to every additional syllable. I have never seen faces more vividly lit up with joy than the faces of the Indian singers. It was to them not only the worship of God, nor an act by which they recalled and commemorated better days, but was besides an exercise of culture, where all they knew of art and letters was combined and expressed."*

Despite the desolate appearance of the ruins and the occupation of the mission grounds by squatters, the Carmel mission had not been completely forgotten by the church after the act of secularization appeared to mark its demise. For years before the United States government turned the property back to the church, occasional services of worship were conducted there for the natives who lived in the valley. Fr. Villarasa, a Dominican friar who was rector of the Monterey parish from 1850 to 1854, had first come over to say mass within the ruins of the former mission church. Fr. Cajetano Sorrentini, Villarasa's successor in the Monterey parish, continued this practice. In 1856 Sorrentini, with some of his parishioners, made the first attempt to locate the burial place of Junípero Serra by digging trenches within the church walls.

According to the report that Fr. Sorrentini made to his

---

*The native choir was accompanied by Juan Onesimo on the violin, which the padres had taught him to play. He took his violin with him when the mission was closed at the time of secularization, and his heirs have returned it to the mission where it is displayed in the mission museum.

bishop, the Rt. Rev. Joseph Sadoc Alemany, on March 12 of
that year, several vaults were discovered in the nave of the
church which "contained bodies, as many as three in each one
and the greater part of the bodies with religious habits."* It
has been assumed that these were bodies of natives who, for
their special usefulness in the mission affairs, had been admit-
ted to the Lay Order of Franciscans, that of Tertiaries.†
Though members of the layman's order did not always wear
the Franciscan habit, they were generally buried in their
religious garb. The bodies must still be under the floor of the
nave of the church, but the actual location of the vaults has
been lost. Also in the nave, according to Fr. Sorrentini's
report, there was found a vault described as being the tomb of a
governor, his wife and child.

On the day after these discoveries were made, Sorrentini and
his helpers moved their activities to the region of the sanctuary. There, on the left side of the altar, they discovered "a
vault well-sealed" which contained "the remains of a priest
with stole and well vested." Of this momentous discovery
Sorrentini reported, "This encounter of a priest so elegantly
clad, a thing which was not so in the case of the others, made
me believe that finally this was him whom we sought." But
when the searchers were disturbed by squatters who lived
nearby, they hurriedly closed the vault and replaced the
ground cover above it. It was another twenty-nine years before
this vault was reopened and eighty-seven years before the
remains of the priest were definitely and officially identified.

When the Carmel mission property was returned to the

---

*The reports of Fr. Sorrentini, quoted here, are all to be found in an article
by the Rev. James Culleton in *Academy Scrapbook I* (Oct. 1950). Copies
of these *Academy Scrapbooks*, which were published by the Diocese of
Monterey-Fresno, are available in the Diocesan Library in Fresno and in
the Downie Library at the Carmel mission.

---

†Both Harry Downie and his assistant, Richard Mann, are Franciscans of
the Tertiary Order.

church in 1859 it was placed under the control of the Monterey parish, and the next pastor to show a particular concern for it was Fr. Angelo Delfino Casanova, who was appointed to the parish in 1863. He interested himself in the mission immediately and began the custom of saying mass there each year on San Carlos Day as well as at other times. By 1877 he was able to reroof the sacristy with $40 that he had collected for the

A painting of Father Casanova in procession at the baptism of a native child. (Courtesy of the Downie Collection)

purpose. It was in this roofed portion of the ruins that Robert Louis Stevenson attended the service in 1879. Among the occasional services held by Fr. Casanova in this earlier time was the baptism of natives still living in the Carmel Valley. Of one of these baptismal services a painting has been preserved in which old Ventura is shown leading a native child for baptism. Ventura, the blind choir leader mentioned by Stevenson in his description of the mass in the reroofed sacristy, continued to lead the choir at the services until his death. Also shown in that picture, standing alongside Fr. Casanova, is a bearded James Meadows and his wife, Loretta.

In 1879 Casanova began to charge tourists an admission fee of ten cents to visit the mission ruins. All profits were to be used exclusively for further restoration of the church building. In the account book he made the note, "When this will be possible God knows," after he had added up the first year's receipts to a total of $11.75!

Within the next year, however, the whole picture in Monterey was to change in a manner that brought new hope for the eventual restoration of the Carmel mission buildings. Robert Louis Stevenson had viewed this new development with alarm as he wrote in 1880, "The Monterey of last year exists no longer. A huge hotel has sprung up in the desert by the railway."

But the cause of Stevenson's fears for Monterey proved to be a boon to the Carmel mission. The management of the great new Del Monte Hotel on the outskirts of Monterey advertised a Seventeen Mile Drive to include a visit to the ruined mission, "one of the best in style and material to be seen in California." The mission visit became a highlight of the trip and soon Fr. Casanova was receiving donations far in exces of the admission fee, increased to fifteen cents, as the tourists contributed to collections for the repair of the mission buildings. Many of those who came to see the mission were moved to make individual gifts to the restoration fund.

At this time the Carmel mission also received widespread publicity from one whose novel, *Ramona*, was a best seller throughout the United States. In 1880 Helen Hunt Jackson made a tour of the California missions with Henry Sandham, an illustrator who made sketches of the missions as they visited them. Of Carmel, Junípero Serra's own mission, Jackson wrote, "Father Junipero sleeps on the spot where he labored and died. His grave is under the ruins of the beautiful stone

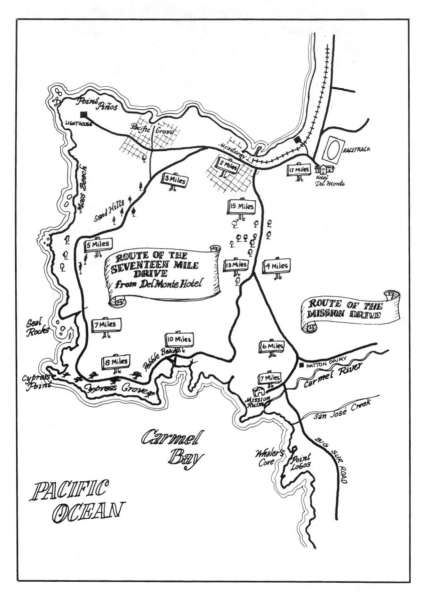

Map of the original Seventeen Mile Drive and Mission Drive. (Prepared by Joe Pierre)

church of his mission, the church which he saw only in ardent and longing fancy.* It was perhaps the most beautiful, though not the grandest, of the mission churches; and its ruins have today a charm far exceeding all the others."

She left a firsthand report of the ruins as she saw them: "The fine yellow tint of the stone, the grand and unique contour of the arches, the beautiful star-shaped window in the front, the simple yet effective lines of carving on pilaster and pillar and doorway, the symmetrical Moorish tower and dome, the worn steps leading up to the belfry—all make a picture whose beauty, apart from the hallowed associations, is enough to hold one spellbound. Reverent nature has rebuilt with grass and blossoms even the crumbling window-sills, across which the wind blows free from the ocean beyond."†

As her book *Ramona* had revived interest in the California missions, so Jackson's strong words regarding the condition of the Carmel mission must have had an influence on those who read her comments: "The roof of the church long ago fell in; its doors have stood open for years; and the fierce sea-gales have been sweeping in, piling sands until a greater part of the floor is covered with solid earth on which every summer grasses grow high enough to cut with sickles. . . . It is a disgrace to both the Catholic Church and the State of California that this grand old ruin, with its sacred sepulchres, should be left to crumble away. If nothing is done to protect and save it, one short hundred years more will see it a shapeless wind-swept mound of sand. . . . The grave of Junipero Serra may be buried centuries

---

*This shows that Jackson knew well the history of the Carmel stone church which was begun under the supervision of Fr. Lasuén nine years after the death of Serra.

---

†Helen Hunt Jackson's visits to the California missions were described in her *Glimpses of California and the Missions* (1883/1903). The quotations given here regarding the Carmel mission are to be found on pages 43 and 47 of that work.

A drawing by Henry Sandham of the interior of the Carmel mission ruins as visited by Helen Hunt Jackson in 1880. (From *Glimpses of California and the Missions*)

deep and its very place forgotten; yet his name will not perish, nor his fame suffer. But for the men of the country whose civilization he founded [California], and of the Church whose faith he so glorified, to permit his burial place to sink into oblivion, is a shame indeed!"

But Serra's burial place was not to sink into oblivion. On January 24, 1882, Fr. Casanova, Cristiano Machado, who was the custodian at Carmel, and other helpers made their attempt to identify the interment of the founder of the mission. Making an opening at the left side of the sanctuary area in the church ruins, workmen struck a board at a depth of about three feet, then a tomb on which slabs of stone had been placed. One of the stone slabs at the foot of the coffin had broken and the redwood board above it had given away so that the lower part of the coffin was filled with dirt. However, the report in a newspaper of the day was that "the upper part and its contents were in a splendid state of preservation."* Realizing the importance of his discovery, Casanova replaced the stone and wood covering over the closed coffin until such time as he could have the church cleared of debris in preparation for a public opening.

On July 3 of that year all was made ready for such an opening. Many people were present for the public occasion, including a contingent of St. Patrick Cadets from San Francisco and reporters from several newspapers of the area and as far away as San Francisco. Fr. Casanova read the burial records of the four priests buried in the church, the Franciscans Serra, Crespí, and Lasuén, who had directed the Carmel mission before their deaths, and Lopez, a young Franciscan who was at the mission when he died, so was buried with the others in the chancel of the church. Three vaults were dis-

---

*Quoted from an article which appeared in the *Monterey Argus* on January 28, 1882. Other accounts were published in the *San Francisco Chronicle*, February 6, 1882 and the *San Francisco Evening Post*, February 17, 1882.

covered, all filled with dirt, and in these were found four skeletons, according to Casanova's report. The redwood coffins were reported to be well preserved and the skeletons in a good state of preservation with a stole in place on each, showing that these were indeed the remains of the four Franciscan padres.

The opening of the tombs in the chancel of the church by Casanova, July 3, 1882. (Courtesy of the Downie Collection)

No attempt was made to identify the skeletons specifically, this being left to a more careful study which was made in 1943 when the graves were opened under official supervision. Unfortunately the stoles were removed from the remains by Fr. Casanova and given out as relics to some of those present on that occasion. By the greatest good fortune, however, the stole that Fr. Casanova presented to Cristiano Machado, the caretaker of the mission ruins, has been preserved. After passing through several hands and being kept at a nearby parish, it has been returned to Carmel where Harry Downie has placed it on display in the room outside Serra's reconstructed cell.

In time it was to be found that Fr. Casanova was more interested in the drama of his opening of the graves than in exactness in reporting what he found within the vaults. On the

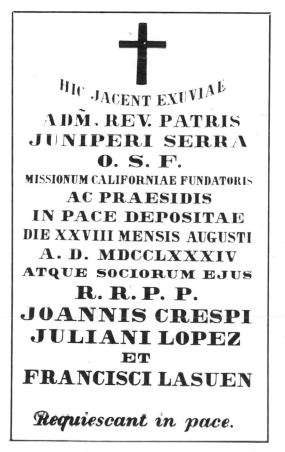

The memorial plaque placed on the wall of the chancel by Father Casanova. (Courtesy of the Downie Collection)

occasion of the 1943 supervised inspection of the burial sites, it was found that there were six bodies within the vaults, including one of a child, instead of four as Casanova had reported. For a time this presented quite a mystery but after a careful search of records the explanation was found and the extra bodies identified. As if to make sure that his secret would be kept, Casanova had raised the level of the chancel floor in 1884 with a seven-inch slab of concrete. Above this he placed the original stones which had covered the coffins in the vaults. So the graves were now covered with twelve inches of concrete and stone. He then placed a memorial plaque on the side wall of the sanctuary above the burial vaults, reading (translated): "Here lie the remains of Administrator Rev. Father Junipero Serra, O. [Order of] S. [Saint] F. [Francis], of Missions of California Founder, And Presidente, in peace interred, day 28 of month August A. [Anno] D. [Domini] 1784 and Associates of his, R.R.P.P. [Reverend Fathers] Juan Crespi, Julian Lopez and Francisco Lasuen. May they rest in peace." This stone was removed from the wall in 1943 when each grave was marked with the name, or names, of the padres buried therein. The stone plaque was then taken down from the wall, there being no further need for it there.

Though it may be that Fr. Casanova was more interested in publicity than in exactness of records, it was the publicity that brought in the funds required for the first reroofing of the Carmel mission church. In 1883 the Bishop of Los Angeles, the Rt. Rev. Francis Mora, made the substantial contribution of $500 and the campaign for the rebuilding was well on its way. In the next year a group of prominent citizens of the state of California joined Fr. Casanova in an appeal for the "Restoration of the Old Mission Church of San Carlos, Carmelo Valley." Addressed "To the people of California" that they should help by their contributions "to commemorate the one hundredth anniversary of the death of her first pioneer, the Founder of the Indian Missions, Padre Junipero Serra."

# Centennial of Padre Junipero Serra.

## Restoration of the Old Mission Church of San Carlos, Carmelo Valley.

## To the People of California.

On the 28th of August, next, California will commemorate the one hundredth anniversary of the death of her first Pioneer, the Founder of the Indian Missions, PADRE JUNIPERO SERRA.

After a long life of sufferings, sacrifices and hard labor, in the service of his beloved Indian flocks, this venerable priest yielded up his spirit to God, and his body was laid at rest under the stone flags of the old church of San Carlos, in Carmelo valley, the scene of his labors and death.

The Mission of San Carlos, first established at Monterey on the 3d of June, 1770, and removed to Carmelo in December of the same year, was the second Mission founded in Upper California by FATHER SERRA, President of the Franciscan Missions.

Of the twenty-one Missions established in California a few are well preserved, others are in ruins, and of some not a vestige is left to mark the spot where they once stood. The most picturesque and poetic of these historic landmarks of our State, and the noblest work of PADRE SERRA is the old stone church of San Carlos, at Carmelo, and it is a sad spectacle and a reproach to California to see this venerable pile through neglect and apathy slowly crumbling into dust.

Inexorable Time had laid his finger on this relic of religion and civilization, and was levelling it to earth, until, quite recently, the Rev. Angelo D. Casanova, the Pastor of Monterey, undertook to stop the work of destruction, and preserve to California this monument of the life and labors of the venerable PADRE SERRA and his last resting place, and also that of some of his co-laborers in the Missions and of a few of the early Governors of California.

The restoration of the old church is going on. Already over $4,000 have been expended on it and the total cost is estimated at about $15,000.

It is hoped that the work will be completed by the 28th of August next, and that the centennial anniversary of the death of the energetic Pioneer will see his work as it stood when his body was laid away under the flags.

We now make an appeal to the people of California, irrespective of creed, to pay a tribute of respect to the memory of this venerable man, by assisting with their means in the restoration of the old stone pile, that it may stand, through coming ages, a monument over the grave of one whom we revere, respect and love.

> "Such graves as his are pilgrim shrines,
> Shrines to no code or creed confined,
> The Delphian vales, the Palestines,
> The Meccas of the mind."

We ask Californians to help this undertaking by forming committees in every town, and forward their collections to Father Casanova, at Monterey; that this building, one of the first fruits of civilization in our beloved State, may be restored, and the centennial anniversary of JUNIPERO SERRA's death commemorated in a manner worthy of the good Pioneer priest.

Announcement of the appeal for funds to rebuild the Carmel mission. (Courtesy of the Downie collection)

His Excellency. George Stoneman, Gov. of California.
Hon. Washington Bartlett, Mayor of San Francisco.
Hon. Geo. C. Perkins, Ex-Gov.
Hon. P. H. Burnett, Ex-Gov.
Hon. Wm. Irwin, Ex-Gov.
Hon. J. G. Downey, Ex-Gov.
Hon. V. E. Howard, Superior Judge.
Hon. Jno. Mansfield, Ex-Lieut. Gov.
Hon. E. E. Thorn, Mayor of Los Angeles.
Hon. C. T. Ryland.
H. H. Bancroft, Esq.
Jos. G. Eastland, Esq.
James R. Kelly, Esq.
T. B. Bishop, Esq.
D. Callaghan, Esq., Pres. First National Bank.
Prof. Joseph Le Conte, University of California.
Prof. E. W. Hilgard, University of California.
John T. Doyle, Esq.
Hon. Thos. Ashworth.
Hon. John Shirley.
G. K. Fitch, Esq.
Prof. Geo. Davidson, Coast Survey.
F. S. Wensinger, Esq.
D. J. Oliver, Esq.
A. S. Hallidie, Esq.
P. C. Molloy, Esq.
James Enright, Esq., Santa Clara.
Gen. M. G. Vallejo, Sonoma.

G. R. B. Hayes, Esq.
Hon. W. T. Wallace.
F. A. A. Belinge, M. D.
Hon. J. F. Sullivan, Sup. Judge.
James J. McDonnell, Esq.
Francis Buckley, Esq., San Francisco.
D. M. Delmas, Esq.
John A. Stanly, Esq.
James Murphy, M. D.
Hon. P. W. Murphy.
Hon. H. W. Smith, Sup. Judge, Los Angeles.
Hon. R. F. Del Valle, State Senator.
Hon. A. F. Coronel, Ex-State Treasurer.
J. W. Hellman, Esq., Pres. F. & M. Bank, Los Angeles.
Hon. J. G. Estudillo, Ex-State Treasurer.
L. Loeb, Esq., Vice French Consul.
A. E. Sepulveda, Esq., County Auditor, Los Angeles.
L. C. Goodwin, Esq., Vice Pres. F. & M. Bank.
N. A. Covarrubias, Esq.
O. W. Childs, Esq., Los Angeles.
W. H. Workman, Esq. "
Albert Kinney, Esq. "
A. W. Potts, Esq. "
S. M. White, Esq. Dist. Attorney, Los Angeles.
James Kays, Esq. County Treasurer, "
Albert Stevens, Esq. City Attorney, "
R. S. Den, M. D., Los Angeles.
J. S. Griffin, M. D. "

Contributions may be sent direct to Rev. Father Angelo D. Casanova, V. F., Monterey, or to First National Bank, San Francisco; Donohoe & Kelly's Bank, San Francisco; The Nevada Bank of San Francisco; Commercial & Savings Bank of San Jose; F. & M. Bank, Los Angeles; or to collectors authorized by Father Casanova.

The list of sponsors for the appeal for funds for the Carmel mission in 1884. (Courtesy of the Downie Collection)

Needed was "about $15,000" in addition to the "$4,000 that has been expended" in order to restore the church building. Included among the fifty-six signers of the appeal were the Governor of California, four ex-Governors, and the mayors of San Francisco and Los Angeles. Contributions were to be made to the banks in San Francisco, San Jose and Los Angeles as well as to Fr. Casanova directly.

With the funds that were received from this appeal the ceiling of the church was restored above wooden arches which replaced the fallen stone arches. The wooden replacements rested on the original stone pilasters, still standing, which divided the four wall sections. The wooden arches, unlike the elliptical stone arches which they replaced, had quarter round corners leading to a flat ceiling which was supported by transverse beams resting on the side walls which had been raised

The interior of the church as rebuilt by Father Casanova's efforts. (Courtesy of the Downie Collection)

with thirty-three inches of adobe construction. The original elliptical shape was preserved, however, in the ceiling of the chancel and above the choir loft in the rear of the church. When the flat ceiling over the nave was removed at the time of the final rebuilding of the church and the whole ceiling returned to its original elliptical form, one of the flattened wooden arches was preserved and may be seen today in the museum to the right of the church doors.

Over the cement slab in the chancel Fr. Casanova replaced the tiles with the same type as the original ones and he installed a new white marble altar. In the niche in which the altar stood he cut two windows and decorated the niche walls with a sky and star effect. The crucifix which had been listed in the 1834 inventory was returned to Carmel from Monterey, where it had been carefully preserved, and placed over the altar in the rebuilt Carmel church. For a distance of about twenty-five feet from the chancel the earthen floor of the nave was covered with planking and a rebuilt pulpit was placed on the original base that hung upon the right wall.

Though the ceiling had been flattened inside the church, the new roof which was placed over it was raised to a peak seventeen feet higher than the original. With shingles replacing the tiles which had covered the church building, the high pitched shingle roof completely destroyed the beauty of the Spanish style of architecture. This departure, which was probably made to follow the gothic style of church building which was in vogue at that time, did serve to preserve the building from further deterioration until such time as builders with a better architectural sense could return it to its original form and beauty.

All was complete by August 28, 1884, the hundredth anniversary of the death of Junípero Serra, with the chair in place in the sanctuary to receive the bishop for the rededication of the building. For the occasion a large crowd gathered from Monterey and the ranches of Carmel Valley as well as from the new village of Carmel-by-the-Sea which was growing near the mission grounds. In this new town a street was to be named for Casanova as well as for the padres prominent in the history of the Carmel mission, Junipero and Serra (two streets), Crespí, Palóu, Lasuén, and even Lopez. Archbishop Joseph Alemany, who had been the Bishop of Monterey when Fr. Sorrentini had made the first identification of the location of Serra's grave in 1856, was present to rededicate the mission church of San Carlos Borromeo as one of his last acts before retirement.

Fr. Casanova established a regular schedule of masses in the rebuilt Carmel mission which was providing a growing congregation as a part of the Monterey parish. He continued to serve as the rector of the Monterey parish until his death in

The crowd gathered for the rededication of the Carmel mission church on August 28, 1884. (Courtesy of the Monterey County Library Collection)

1893 and was buried in the Pacheco crypt of the San Carlos Church, Monterey, on March 15, 1893.

Father Raymond Mestres, who succeeded Casanova at Monterey, continued to take an active interest in the Carmel portion of his parish. Of his activities in the early years of his pastorate there he wrote to his bishop, "When I came here in 1893 nearly all the adobe walls and buildings around the church proper were private property or belonging to the county. On several occasions I have prevented these adobe walls and buildings from being carted away by the county road masters who were going to use them to fill depressions and holes in the county roads. By degrees I succeeded in getting all those adobe walls back to the diocese and they are now ours."*

The Carmel mission church surrounded by the adobe walls of the mission complex in Fr. Mestres' time. (Courtesy of the Downie Collection)

*Letter from Fr. Mestres to Bishop Cantwell, Monterey, July 12, 1919.

That the area to the left of the church entrance was filled with the ruined adobe walls of the old mission buildings is to be seen from photographs of Mestres' time, but surely these were on the land returned by the Federal Government in 1859. And one wonders what sort of road base the adobe material would make. Mestres' letter is a bit difficult to understand at this late date.

The one place where the original adobe walls of the old mission buildings can still be seen is on the outer wall of the present day chapel. The original adobe building in this place was first built for the blacksmith and carpenter shop and was probably used in later years as a hospice for mission visitors. When this part of the mission buildings was rebuilt in 1946 to serve as a chapel for the daily mass and occasional services for small groups, the outer wall was rebuilt upon an existing portion of the original wall and protected by a porch. In the reconstruction the portion of original wall that was used was left unplastered so that the early type of construction could be observed. In this original method of building, as can be seen there, a course of flat stones was placed between the courses of adobe bricks in order to strengthen the wall and to hold the plaster covering.

Continuing his interest in the restoration of the Carmel mission, Fr. Mestres sought the support of the secretary to King Alfonso of Spain, the Spanish ambassador to Washington, as well as the members of the Spanish families in California and the chapters of the Knights of Columbus. Shortly before the outbreak of the war in 1914 he had raised enough money to buy the piece of property adjoining the mission church, measuring seventy by eighty feet. This would enable him to rebuild the entire quadrangle as it was in the mission period and in its original location. But war made any construction at that time impossible so his plans had to be set aside.

Mestres' report to his bishop in 1919, after the war had ended, showed that his interest had not waned: "I have during the last twelve years of my pastorate here devoted considerable time to the study of the original plan made by the Spanish authorities here in 1773–1785 of all buildings connected with said [Carmel] *Mission. I have gathered every old painting and map from those days that would give a more accurate idea of* the location of the original buildings."

On November 23 of that year Mestres marked the 106-year anniversary of Serra's birth with a groundbreaking for a planned reconstruction of all the mission buildings according to elaborate plans made for him by Bernard Maybeck, who had designed the Palace of Fine Arts for the Panama Pacific Exposition of 1915. The ceremonies at the groundbreaking for this immense project began with a mass in the partially restored mission church. Fr. Mestres wore the very chasuble, maniple and stole formerly worn by Junípero Serra at mission services and used the same chalice and paten which Serra had used so many years before.* These and other treasures which had been carefully preserved in the Monterey church can be

A sketch made by Jo Mora of the projected plan for the mission reconstruction according to plans made for Fr. Mestres by Bernard Maybeck. (Courtesy of the Downie Collection)

---

*The vestments and vessels from Serra's day were brought back to Carmel by Harry Downie. He built the exhibit cases around the walls of the Sar-cophagus Chapel and placed the glass front at the altar steps to protect the vessels and other mission treasures to be seen there.

seen today in the Sarcophagus Chapel, the room for which ground was broken on that day.

The state secretary for the Mission Restoration Fund in 1919 was Maria Antonia Field, a fourth generation member of the Munras family which was, in 1961, to give the Munras Museum that stands behind the mission church, beyond the altar wall. The Munras family had received large grants of land

Lady Maria Antonia Field wearing the decoration that she received from the King of Spain in recognition of her work in perpetuating Spanish-California history. (Courtesy of the Downie Collection)

in the Monterey area, and Miss Field's father, a Monterey banker who married into the family, had wisely held onto the land. Prominent in international social circles, the family had once fenced off a portion of their Rancho Laguna Seca in order that it should serve as a game preserve, in anticipation of a visit from the King of Spain. That was in the late twenties.

His Highness did not actually arrive in this area on that occasion but in 1931 he did grant to Maria Antonia Field the title of "Lady of the Royal Order and Grand Cross of Isabella the Catholic" for her work in perpetuating Spanish-California history. This was one of the last acts of the king before he was overthrown in the Spanish Revolution. Because this honor carried the title *Excelentisima* in Spain, Maria used the title "Lady Field" as the nearest English equivalent. She was later to explain that she was denied the court investiture to which the honor entitled her because the king abdicated on the day after she was decorated. Maria left Spain on the same Pullman as the queen, princesses and other members of the royal court.

On October 21, 1921 the cornerstone was laid for the building which Fr. Mestres expected to be the first in the total mission reconstruction. The ceremonies began on this occasion with the baptism of Alejandro, Bertoldi and Juanito Onesimo, three descendants of one of the natives who had been baptized by Fr. Serra. The Serra vestments and vessels were used again in the celebration of the mass. Following this an outdoor pageant depicting the early years of the mission was enacted near the northeast wall of the church. Then two of the Carmel natives were called forward to place the cornerstone, Alejandro Onesimo, one of the newly baptized, and his father Manuel, who had been baptized at the mission before secularization. Amidst the ruined adobe walls of the old buildings the cornerstone was laid for the rebuilding of the mission quadrangle. Unfortunately the construction of the two small buildings on either side of the church entrance was all that Mestres was able to accomplish of his plans for the restoration. Within

Manuel and Alejandro Onesimo bearing the cornerstone for the 1921 reconstruction. (Courtesy of the Downie Collection)

the church he had a cement floor laid and he arranged for the return of the Stations of the Cross to their original places on the walls as well as some of the other old paintings which had been rescued from the church at the time of secularization. But Mestres will always be remembered best for the outstanding Serra sarcophagus, for which he was responsible.

He conceived the idea of the sarcophagus for Fr. Serra like those in European churches and believed that he had found a sculptor equal to the task when he saw the heroic statue of Cervantes in the Golden Gate Park in San Francisco. He met the sculptor, Jo Mora (Joseph Jacinto Mora), through George Barron, Curator of the de Young Museum in the park. The priest and artist at once struck a strong friendship, we are told. Mora caught Mestres' enthusiasm for the project which he expressed in a letter that he wrote to Senator Phelan of San Francisco in 1920: "I am here to 'settle up' one of the most important and interesting commissions I have ever been given. It is to execute the Sarcophagus for Father Junipero Serra and the three Franciscans buried beside him in the Carmel Mission. Could anything be grander for the sculptor who loves California—or fraught with more romantic and sentimental possibilities? I'm girding my loins for the supreme professional effort in my life."

A view of the Sarcophagus Chapel as completed to the left of the church entrance. The building to the right was the first built in Mestres' time. (Courtesy of the Downie Collection)

It was intended, at the beginning, to place the sarcophagus above the graves in the church, but as the design progressed it became evident that the work planned by Mora would be too large for that location. Plans were then made to use the building for which ground had been broken to the left of the church door as a chapel to hold the sarcophagus. Some tourists are surprised to find that the grave of Serra is within the chancel of the church while his sarcophagus ('stone coffin') is some distance away and outside the church door. But there is a tradition for the sculptured sarcophagus to be apart from the actual burial place. In St. Peter's Cathedral in Rome and the church of Santa Cruz in Florence, as in many other European churches, the sarcophagus will be found to be empty of a body, the actual interment having been in the crypt below.

Jo Mora first made a small scale model of the work as he planned it and when this was approved he moved into a studio on the mission grounds where he formed the full scale sculpture in plaster. Fr. Mestres approved each stage of the plaster work, which was complete within the year. The figures were then sent to New York for casting while Mora continued to work on the bas-reliefs that decorate the sides of the base. Like many artists before and after him, Mora fell in love with Carmel and continued to live in the new town until his death.

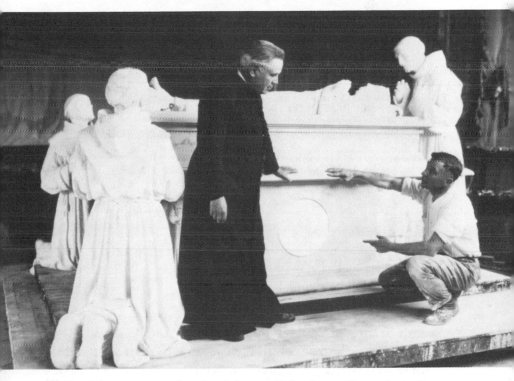

Father Mestres approving the plaster model as formed by sculptor Jo Mora. (Courtesy of the Hathaway Collection)

The unveiling of the completed sarcophagus was set for October 12, 1924 because that was the date nearest to the time of the annual pilgrimage on which the Duke of Alba could be present to represent the King of Spain. A crowd of approximately thirteen hundred, according to newspaper reports, filled the church and the Sarcophagus Chapel, for which Mora had also carved the great wooden altar cross, and overflowed into the courtyard between the chapel and the church building. The ceremonies began with a solemn high mass in the church followed by the procession of the principals, servers and choir to the chapel where the sarcophagus was veiled with three flags, the American, the Spanish, and the Papal.

A part of the crowd gathered for the dedication of the Serra sarcophagus and chapel on October 12, 1924. (Courtesy of the Monterey County Library Collection)

James Phelan, former mayor of San Francisco and United States Senator from California, withdrew the American flag and spoke a few words of tribute to Junípero Serra, as did the others who participated in the unveiling. The Duke of Alba, the Marquis de Viani, took away the Spanish flag, while Fr. Mestres and Monsignor Gleason, who had preached the sermon at the mass, withdrew the Papal flag. Then there was a roll call of the twenty-one California missions that had been established by Serra, Crespí, Palóu and Lasuén. As the representatvie of each mission answered the roll call he stepped forward to lay a wreath of flowers at the base of the sarcophagus and to say a few words to honor Fr. Serra.

The Serra sarcophagus is one of the finest pieces of its sort to be seen in America, and is on a par with the best that the European churches have to offer. The bronze figure of Serra lies atop in an attitude of repose rather than death, clad in Franciscan habit with his stole, crucifix, cord and rosary. The bare feet of the padre rest on a grizzly bear cub, representing the State of California to whose civilization Serra contributed so greatly. The figure rests on a base of travertine stone measuring eight by twelve feet.

On the frieze which runs around the stone base Mora carved an ornamental molding representing persons and events in the history of the California missions. On one side is pictured a procession of soldiers and settlers on horses followed by loaded pack mules, reminiscent of the Portolá and Anza expeditions. On the other side is a representation of natives attacking a mission, as did happen on a few occasions (but never at Carmel), along with scenes picturing the baptism of a native child and a celebration of the mass. Below this frieze are, on one side, panels showing natives and Spanish workers with a medallion of Pope Pius VI between, and on the other, panels with monks and soldiers and a medallion of King Charles III of Spain between.

At the head of the sarcophagus and on each side by the foot of it are three lifesize bronze figures wearing the Franciscan habit and posed in an attitude of prayer. As stated by Mora in his letter to Senator Phelan, the three figures around the monument were designated to represent the three Franciscans buried with Serra in the chancel of the church. But whenever I view this beautiful work which memorializes the Franciscan

Jo Mora, the sculptor, standing beside the sarcophagus that he created for Junípero Serra in its place in the Sarcophagus Chapel. (Courtesy of the Hathaway Collection)

padre who established the California mission system, I see the three figures as his three faithful companions in the mission task: Juan Crespí, who studied under Serra at Lull University on Mallorca and was his faithful companion until his death, shortly before his master's; Francisco Palóu, who also studied under Serra at Lull University, then came with him to Mexico, worked with him until Serra's own death and then wrote a biography of his master*; and Fermin Francisco de Lasuén, a fellow Spaniard who took over Serra's task and completed what Serra called his "Rosary of Missions."

---

*An attempt was made in 1955 to find the remains of Fr. Palóu and bring them to Carmel for interment here. He had died in Queretero, Mexico, and was buried in the chancel of the Convento de la Santa Cruz there. But his bones, along with those of several others buried in the chancel, were placed in an ossuary when a new floor was laid in the Convento with the result that it was not possible to identify the remains of Palóu.

## Bibliographical Note

Some information regarding the first years of the rebirth of the Carmel mission is to be found in Appendix F of *Mission San Carlos Borromeo* by Fr. Zephyrin Engelhardt, O.F.M. A more complete record is to be found in a thesis written by Sister Maria Celeste Pagliarulo, S.N.D., titled *The Restoration of Mission San Carlos Borremeo, Carmel, California*, a copy of which is to be found in the Harry Downie Library at the Carmel mission together with other valuable records of the period covered in this chapter.

# FIVE

# The Rebuilding
# of the Mission Basilica
# San Carlos Borromeo

he Carmel church which was reborn under the
Monterey pastors, Frs. Casanova and Mestres, stood within
the walls of the mission church but had little else in common
with the original mission buildings. In placing a roof upon the
walls of the mission church Fr. Casanova had replaced the
elliptical stone ceiling of Lasuén's church with a flat wooden
ceiling that had quarter-round arched ends to rest on the
ancient walls. Above the ceiling he raised a high peaked roof
which followed the then current Gothic style of church
building but which did not fit the Spanish style of the original
building. Inside the church he raised the level of the chancel
floor and broke into the old wall in the cove behind the altar in
order to add two incongruous windows there.

Father Mestres, who had plans for the reconstruction of the
whole of the original compound, ended up simply adding a
small priest's house to the right of the church door, where no
building stood in mission days, and by replacing the mission
hospice to the left of the door with a chapel for the Serra
sarchophagus. In this chapel he did replace the first unit of the
original buildings of the compound and he did follow a
simplified mission style with tiled roof of a proper low pitch.

The Carmel church as it appeared in Father Mestres' day. (Courtesy of the Downie Collection)

But in front of the forecourt he placed a picket fence with a wagon gate framed in ranch style so that a visitor approaching would see what appeared to be a large ranch chapel with a wooden cattle fence and gate. He would be surprised to see no other ranch buildings around but only the remains of many half-fallen adobe walls to the left of the area in front of the chapel.

In place of the mission compound a modern parish house, Crespí Hall, had been built in the middle of what had been the large square patio that in mission days had been surrounded by the dormitories and workshops behind a covered walkway. In 1930 one certainly could not have been faulted for doubting whether the Carmel mission would ever be rebuilt to correspond to its original form and beauty.

Yet the mission was destined to be rebuilt in its original style and grandeur, and that under the guidance of a twentieth century Franciscan. This Franciscan was not to be seen about the buildings in the usual habit, but generally in the garb of a workman, for this member of the Tertiary, the lay order of

Franciscans, was trained not in theology but in cabinet making and in the refinishing of antiques.* Henry John Downie, born August 25, 1903 in San Francisco, was baptized in the Mission Dolores and nurtured in its shadow. There he gained his first knowledge of and interest in the California missions. Having been brought first to Carmel on a visit with his parents soon after the earthquake of 1906, Harry Downie† was to spend many vacations in the little village then growing up among the pines by the sea. At the age of twelve he made a model of the facade of the Carmel mission which he had often visited with his friend, Lawrence Farrel, who sometimes served as a tourist guide there.‡

A view of the compound area of the mission with Crespí Hall in its original location. (Courtesy of the Downie Collection)

---

*Downie was apprenticed in 1919 to the A. T. Hunt cabinet firm which specialized in renovations and reproductions of old Spanish furniture.

†He has long been known by his friends, who are legion, as "Harry" Downie.

‡That model has been kept by Downie and is today in the Harry Downie Library in the mission.

Having become well acquainted during his visits to Carmel with Msgr. Philip Scher, the pastor in Monterey who had charge of the Carmel church, Downie stopped to see him in August 1931 on his way to Santa Barbara. He had planned to set up his own cabinetmaking business in the southern town, but he stayed for a time in Monterey in order to repair some chipped and broken statues for Msgr. Scher. One job led to another until he had repaired and restored enough statues and

Harry Downie at work repairing an ancient figure. (Courtesy of the Downie Collection)

paintings to start a small museum in a room of the Monterey rectory. When his work in Monterey was completed he began to restore objects at the Mission San Carlos in Carmel. His future was determined for he never did establish his cabinet shop. When Msgr. Scher became the Vicar General of the Diocese of Monterey-Fresno he appointed Downie to work at the restoration of the buildings of all the old missions in the diocese with his housing provided in Crespí Hall in Carmel.

Father Michael Murphy, the curate of the Carmel church who was living in the small priest's house built by Fr. Mestres, resented this "intruder" at first. But he soon came to enjoy Harry's cooking and companionship as Harry worked on the old statues, scraping cracked paint, repairing broken bits and carving replacements for limbs and features that were missing. He did the same service for the faded and cracked paintings in the church and began to gather the vestments and vessels that had previously belonged to the Carmel mission for the museum which he was establishing there.

Many of the mission treasures had been preserved at the time of secularization only because they were taken to the Monterey church. Rich vestments sent to Serra and his successors from Mexico, silver candelabra and crosses for the altar and processions, along with Serra's silver chalice and paten, had been carefully preserved by the Monterey rectors for almost a century.

Downie tells the story of the manner in which these treasures were returned to Carmel, where they are housed today in the Sarcophagus Chapel. Strong in his belief that these things rightfully belonged at the Carmel mission, he would accept dinner invitations to the San Carlos rectory in Monterey with a purpose in mind. After the meal, while others were engaged in conversation, he would absent himself from the room and stealthily remove a few of the ancient mission vestments, hanging them with his coat. The vestments would go back to Carmel with Downie when he left. Father James Culleton,

The Sarcophagus Chapel, showing the cabinets for ancient vestments and the original vessels and other silver treasures on the altar.
(Courtesy of the Downie Collection)

then the assistant at the Monterey parish, noticed that some of
the Serra vestments were missing from their place of storage.
He next saw them displayed in the new glass cases which
Downie had made and placed around the walls of Carmel's
Sarcophagus Chapel, where they may be viewed today. It must
be said that the silver treasures now to be seen in that museum
room were willingly returned to Carmel at a later date.

Downie's skill as a cabinetmaker was soon to grow into an
active interest in the construction of the buildings themselves.
In preparation for his task of rebuilding he consulted all the
sources available in order to be sure that his restoration work
should be correct in every detail. He searched through the
annual reports and inventories made from the time that the
mission was founded by Serra, and made photostatic copies of

them for his library in the mission, where they may be consulted today.* Next he sought out the reports of those who had visited the Carmel mission, finding them in Mexico and Spain, as well as in California collections.† Photographs, beginning as early as 1860, were collected and the testimony of old-timers was taken. The natives who survived from mission days related to him in their strange "California Spanish" dialect their experiences at the mission and their recollections of the way things appeared in olden times.

By excavation Downie found in the ground the verification of information that he had received from written and oral sources. Following the evidence of the remains of foundations and the few remaining parts of the adobe walls, he was able to find the original location of all the buildings which bordered the compound. In the construction of the replacement buildings the original foundation lines were followed except that some of the outside walls were moved out in order that the classrooms of the school buildings around the patio might be wider than the dormitories and workrooms which once stood in those locations.

The knowledge that Downie gained of Spanish Colonial construction enabled him to make an authentic reconstruction of the original buildings. His attitude toward the rebuilding of the mission was expressed by him in these words: "In restoration you start with what you find and continue the same way . . . You have to do it the way it was done, putting in all the crooked walls and inaccuracies. You can't have any ideas of your own; you'll fizzle. You've got to follow their ideas.

---

*The inventory dated December 10, 1834 was thirty-nine pages in length and others were of similar length.

---

†In the year 1931 Downie made a four-month journey around the world as a cabinetmaker on a Dollar Liner. He found sources in Spain on this trip and even visited the birthplace of Junípero Serra in Petra on the island of Mallorca.

... The Spanish were excellent craftsmen, but they were after an effect rather than perfection. They could build a straight wall, but a wavy one appealed to them more. A square corner, a straight line—neither looked good to a Spaniard."*

Downie started the reconstruction by building two rooms of the present museum which duplicated the rooms of the original priests' quarters. When this first unit of the north side of the quadrangle was built it was found that the area in front of the church had collected soil through the years until it was higher than the church floor. Whenever there was a heavy rain, as there often is in Carmel winters, the water flowed in the front doors of the church, through the building and out the door by the chancel. The first thing that had to be done, therefore, was to lower this forecourt and to install a drain to take the water past the church and out of the quadrangle area. Harry then

The forecourt of the church, showing the first building built by Downie (beside the car) after the courtyard had been lowered and a drain installed. (Courtesy of the Downie Collection)

---

*As quoted in an article in the *Monterey Peninsula Herald* on January 12, 1955.

moved into one room of the first section of the mission buildings which had been rebuilt under his direction and made plans for further reconstruction of the original compound.

The rebuilding of the Carmel mission took on a new impetus when Carmel became a parish in 1933 with Fr. Michael O'Connell as the first pastor. The Spanish mission was destined to be rebuilt by two Irishmen, Downie and O'Connell, for, as Sister Marie wrote in her valuable thesis on the restoration of the mission, "Father O'Connell, the first pastor, shared Downie's vision of a completely restored compound and realized that this unassuming young man was the one capable of doing it. He had complete faith in Downie."* But for all that faith each had in the other, both had a full measure of native temperament. The early years of the Downie-O'Connell partnership in reconstruction is remembered well by Mrs. Xavier Martinez, who moved from Oakland to Carmel at about the time that Fr. O'Connell became the Carmel rector.† Now nearing her ninetieth birthday, Elsie "Pelli" Martinez loves to recall the days of the mission rebuilding as she relates that "they were ever arguing, those two Irishmen, but Harry always won, because he was right, you know."

In addition to his task of making plans for the restoration of the mission buildings and his sharing in the labor of the actual rebuilding, Downie guided tourists through the church. For the sake of atmosphere, the guide often wore a cassock and he found that some of the visitors would address him as "Brother Harry" or "Father Downie." He didn't bother to correct them as long as the vestment tended to arouse interest in the mission and to stimulate visitors' desire to make monetary contributions for the rebuilding.

---

*The Restoration of Mission San Carlos Borromeo, Carmel, California, 1931-1967 by Sister Marie Celeste Pagliarulo, S.N.D. (1968), page 36.

†Mrs. Martinez is the widow of the San Francisco and Oakland based Mexican artist whose work can be seen in the Oakland Art Museum and elsewhere in museum collections.

Harry Downie and Fr. O'Connell supervising the raising of an adobe wall in the rebuilding of the mission buildings. (Courtesy of the Hathaway Collection)

It was at this time that he started the ceremony of the descent from the cross as a part of the Good Friday services. On the large life-size crucifix above the altar he had affixed the figure of the Christus to the cross with nails piercing the hands which he had carved. On Good Friday he would raise a black ladder behind the cross and mount it in his black vestments as the priest led the procession by the twelve Stations of the Cross. Before the procession reached the altar he would withdraw the nails, holding the figure on the cross with bands of cloth. As the priest approached the altar Downie would lower the figure from the cross by the bands until it rested in an incumbent position on a pallet which had been placed at the foot of the cross. The pallet with the carved figure upon it was then carried back through the church and deposited in the side chapel where it remained until Easter morning. This pageant, which represented the sort of "acted out" teaching of the old padres, was continued until 1975. When Downie felt that he could not handle it himself, he no longer had the Good Friday ceremony carried out. Those who have come to Carmel on Good Friday since 1975 are therefore deprived of an opportunity to share in a unique experience.

Money for the restoration began to increase once Carmel became a parish. Pageants, charity balls, drawings, ballet performances and a horse show were held as means of raising money for the rebuilding of the mission. In 1934 a dramatic pageant was a part of the sesquicentennial anniversary of the death of Serra, made to coincide with the Monterey Fiesta, which always brought many tourists to the area. The pageant,

The interior of the church with Downie's decorations and crucifix before the old ceiling was replaced. (Courtesy of the Downie Collection)

titled "The Apostle of California," was written by George Marion, an actor, director and producer of plays in New York for twenty-five years before moving to Hollywood, then retiring to Carmel. It was presented nightly from August 24 through 28. The latter date had been designated "Junipero Serra Day" by the California State Senate. Marion took the role of Serra in the production, which was presented in an outdoor amphitheatre built near the mission. The amphitheatre seated 1,600 persons, and Downie constructed it out of material which was later to be used for the new ceiling in the church.

Between 1930 and 1935 a total of only $8,150 had been raised for the restoration of the church, a job which would cost many times that amount. But in October 1935, the raising of funds for the work had been put on a more solid foundation with the establishment of "The Carmel Mission Restoration Committee." Bishop Scher was asked to be a member of the committee and to give his permission for the campaign to raise sufficient funds for the task before it. Two years earlier grating sounds heard in the church were found to be caused by the movement of the stone extension which Casanova had added to the facade. This extension, which had been built there to form the gable for the high-pitched shingle roof, was now leaning outward. Casanova's stone gable had been set atop the arch of the original facade without any tie-rods to hold the new construction atop the old. Now the new gable was discovered to have pulled six inches away from the shingle roof. The bishop realized that the removal of Casanova's stone gable and the cutting back of his roof at an angle from the original facade, which was done at that time, provided only a temporary solution to the problem. He was, therefore, happy to concur in the plans for the general restoration of the ailing building.

Bishop Scher sanctioned the raising of money by the Carmel Mission Restoration Fund on October 10, 1935, and issued this statement:

A view of the mission with Casanova's stone gable removed from the church front and the shingle roof cut back at an angle from the original facade. (Courtesy of the Downie Collection)

"At the present time the old roof is in a miserable condition and must be replaced. This consideration has determined me to grant the request of the Committee for a campaign to raise the needed sum. This permission I give at this time, but I wish it clearly understood that this shall be the last general campaign for reconstruction funds. I see no reason to doubt that once the old memorial is well roofed, the local authorities with the aid of tourists and pageant receipts shall be able not only to maintain the place in good order, but in time to rebuild the quadrangle along its original lines. It is most important that the roof be replaced just as it was originally. An exact replica has therefore been prepared by Mr. Harry Downie. This has formed the guide for the plans which are already complete."*

The professional money raiser who was hired by the committee to conduct the campaign for $5,000 to start the new roof was a disappointment; less than half that amount was

*Quoted by Sister Marie in her thesis, page 39.

raised through the giving of private individuals. Yet the proceeds from a ball and card party at the Hotel Del Monte and from the annual Serra festivals, together with almost $2,000 from parish funds, did bring in a total of $6,586.60 by the time the new roof was ready to be dedicated. Increases in building costs between the time of planning and time of completion were as prevalent in 1936 as they are at the present time. So by the time of the dedication an additional $5,900 had to be borrowed to pay for the work done on the new ceiling and the incomplete roof. The tiling of the bare roof boards had to be postponed until another $2,000 was found.

The old roof of the church removed in preparation for its replacement with the domed ceiling over the chapel in place. (Courtesy of the Downie Collection)

In preparation for the "razing of the roof," the rooms in which Downie had been living were combined and redecorated to form a temporary Blessed Sacrament Chapel in which services could be held.* This chapel was blessed on March 2, 1936 and the new wooden ceiling arches were being built in Crespí Hall which had been turned into a temporary work-

---

*Downie was married at this time and he moved into a house in Carmel with his wife.

shop. The new arches, which measured forty-two feet across with an upper span of twenty-six feet, followed exactly the arches of the original ceiling, as Downie had been able to trace the end one in the marks left on the wall over the choir loft. By April 15 the arches to support the ceiling had all been prepared and in May the church roof was removed, with tarpaulins placed over the altar and other objects that could not be moved out. Hope that the rain would hold off was in vain, however, for at the end of that month a heavy rain flooded the floor of the roofless church.

The new ceiling of redwood planks resting on the wooden arches rose thirty-three feet from the floor. When the new roof was raised above the ceiling the top of the gable was fifteen feet lower than the shingled roof of 1884 and followed the lines of the original roof of 1797. The appearance of the facade was improved by the filling in of the cracks and crevices which had developed in the more than a century and a half of standing in

The church ceiling being rebuilt in 1936. (Courtesy of the Hathaway Collection)

The service of dedication of the new ceiling and roof which took place on July 5, 1936. (Courtesy of the Downie Collection)

all weather, and by an antique yellow wash. On July 5, 1936 the church, returned to its original appearance, with the original roof line restored and the facade resurfaced, was rededicated.

The three cells which had been built in 1775 to house the padres at the mission were being rebuilt on their original foundations even as the new roof was going on the church. These rooms in the north wing of the mission quadrangle were so reconstructed in their original form that it is hard for the visitor to believe that he is not actually in the original building as he walks through them today. Though Serra's cell, as rebuilt, contains none of the original furnishings, Downie has so followed the description of the cell and its contents as given in Serra's biography written by Fr. Palóu that it does appear just as it did when Serra died there in 1784.

Serra's restored cell was dedicated on August 29, 1937 by Fr. O'Connell. Local natives, including members of the Onesimo family, were among those congregated for the occasion, as well as many who had been involved in the early stages of the reconstruction of the mission. The natives came as pilgrims to the place which had meant so much to their forefathers and mothers, and placed a wreath of flowers on the simple cot in the cell. Lady Maria Antonia Field, who had been active in promoting the rebuilding since the time of Fr. Mestres, laid a wreath on Serra's tomb in the sanctuary of the church. At the mass which followed the dedication, the eulogy of Father Serra was preached by Fr. Augustine Hobrecht, O.F.M., who was the postulator for Serra's beatification. This marked the formal beginning of the cause for beatification of the founder of the California missions.

The next summer a second pageant, "The Rose of Carmel," again written by George Marion, was presented at the mission. A sizable addition to the building fund was made, as many from distant places were attracted to the well-publicized performances. Mrs. Elsie Martinez was one who "bombarded" the newspapers throughout Northern California with stories about the rebuilding of the Carmel mission and the affairs presented there for the building fund. An editor of the *San Francisco Chronicle* who was introduced to Mrs. Martinez at a party in the city is reported to have exclaimed, "So you are the person who sends us an article for the paper every time anyone sneezes at the Carmel mission." But the publicity did work and the rebuilding could be carried forward.

The tile roof went on and the restoration of the padres' quarters was completed with the rebuilding of the padres' kitchen and dining room, together with two rooms to be used as a museum to hold artifacts found in excavations on the grounds and items connected with the mission which had been restored by those who had lovingly cared for them through the years. The library and a tourist entrance were incorporated in

Tiles being placed on the roof of the church. (Courtesy of the Downie Collection)

this section of the rebuilding. Because of his interest in the California missions and his knowledge of their development, Downie has been able to collect material for the most complete museum to be found at any Franciscan mission. For the library he gathered books marked by Fr. Lasuén's mark from all over California and beyond, with the result that the restored mission library now has 80 percent of the volumes collected by Serra and Lasuén.

The next building to be rebuilt was the present rectory on the site of the Spanish soldiers barracks, beginning the reconstruction of the east wing of the quadrangle. The whole of the area of the original compound was carefully excavated in order to make sure that the buildings of the restoration were constructed exactly on the site of the original structures. It was in December 1939 that Downie came across stones laid in a circular form of about four feet in diameter, just outside the covered walkway near the sarcophagus room. In the center of the circle he found small fragments of wood. This intriguing discovery called for more checking of old records and drawings. He found the answer as he read again Palóu's account and studied the drawing made by J. Sykes who had accompanied Vancouver on his visit to the mission in 1794.

Downie had discovered the remains of the cross raised by Serra in 1771 before any building was raised at the Mission San Carlos location. As is evident from the Sykes drawing, in which the site of the stone church is seen in the open area in the middle of the drawing, this was the location of the original Serra cross.* The stones were placed there by Serra and his helpers to hold the cross in place. The wood fragments were the remains of the actual cross which had been made of ten inch-square hand hewn timbers. Downie formed a cross exactly duplicating the Serra cross and placed it where Serra had first raised it. There it is to be seen today, just outside the colonnaded porch by the door to the sarcophagus room.

Harry Downie raising the replacement for the Serra cross. (Courtesy of the Downie Collection)

---

*The Sykes drawing is pictured on page 57 of this book.

At about this time Downie began to renew the forecourt of the church in its original form. In checking the county records he found that the land restored to the Carmel mission in 1859 extended only to the edge of the remaining buildings. All surrounding land still belonged to the Martin ranch which encircled the mission, so that even the courtyard in front of the church door did not belong to the parish. He presented the problem to Carmel Martin, the local lawyer who had been born at the ranch and was now head of the Martin family. Carmel Martin told him that "land around the mission was deeded to the church in 1920" and asked his secretary to find the trust deed in his files. When the record was found it was discovered that the deed had never been recorded, so that the land adjoining the mission building still belonged to the ranch. A new deed was written which granted to the Carmel church all the land around the mission buildings "to the middle of the nearest road" and was then duly recorded.

This gave to the church all the area of the forecourt within the present walls, and also the strip of land alongside Rio Road which today provides parking space for tourists' cars and buses. Also included was sufficient area along Lasuén Drive for Crespí Hall, the Munras Museum, and the convent for the sisters who teach in the school.

The forecourt was then developed in its original form with a fountain in the center, and paths bordered with salvia plants, enclosing beds of many varieties of flowers including the native California poppy. By the walls were planted Wisteria and the everblooming Bougainvillea vines. About this courtyard and inside the patio were planted orange, lemon and olive trees, as well as the native California live oak and redwood, the Monterey cypress, the black wattle from Australia and the yew from Ireland.

Inside the church Downie began to restore the sanctuary floor to its original level by removing the seven inches of concrete that had been added by Fr. Casanova. In doing this he

The forecourt of the Carmel mission church. (Courtesy of the Downie Collection)

came upon the tombs which had been opened first by Fr. Sorrentini, then by Casanova. After glancing into one of the tombs through a small opening that he cut, he resealed the opening until a more formal opening of the tombs could be arranged.

The canonical exhumation of Serra's remains began on September 1, 1943 and continued until December 1. Included in the number of those who participated in the official act were the Very Rev. John Durkin, V.F., as the bishop's delegate, the Rev. Lucien Arvin, M.E.P., as promoter of the faith, the Rev. Constantine Badesen as notary, together with Fr. O'Connell, the rector, and Harry Downie, who were listed as "custodians of the church and sepulchre," with the addition of two "skilled workmen" who were under Downie. The two physicians invited to participate as "skilled anatomical physicians" were Major Richard F. Berg, M.D., from Fort Ord, and Clemens Nagleman, M.D. In all twenty persons witnessed all or part of the exhumation, including Jo Mora, the sculptor of the Serra sarcophagus, George Marion, who had portrayed Serra in the pageants presented at the mission, and Mrs. Mary Goold, the daughter of Cristiano Machado, caretaker of the mission at the time of the 1882 uncovering of the tombs by Father Casanova.*

Downie and his helper, Rafael Torres, had broken the concrete slab over the chancel with a compressor in August so that all was ready on September 1 for the opening of the tombs. On that day the central vault was opened and the coffin therein found to be filled with dirt. When the earth was removed from around the bones a bronze reliquary cross was found in the chest area. This reliquary served to identify the remains as those of Junípero Serra, for on the back of the cross were set nine relics of the blessed Raymond Lull, to whom Serra had shown great devotion.† This cross is to be seen today in a framed case carved by Downie and hanging on the wall outside the rebuilt Serra cell. The cross hands in the case with a mirror behind it so that the nine small reliquaries on the back of the cross may be plainly seen. In the same case is the portion of Serra's stole which Fr. Casanova removed from the coffin in 1882 as well as nails and a piece of wood from the coffin.

In the vault with the Serra coffin were found bones of another skeleton which was believed to be that of Fr. Crespí, whose remains were placed beside Serra's in the central vault in

---

*Also present as observers were the Very Rev. Gregory Wooler, O.F.M., the Rev. Eric O'Brien, O.F.M., the Rev. Maynard Geiger, O.F.M., the Rev. Joseph Pastorelli, O.P., the R، Michael Harding, O.F.M., the Rev. Domain Blaber, O.F.M., and the Kev. Alan McCoy, O.F.M., as well as the Rev. D. Curtin and the Rev. McAuliffe of the U.S. Army. Sergeant Joseph Rinoyas of the U.S. Army acted as the official photographer.

---

†It was at the Lullian University in Palma, Mallorca, that Serra had taught philosophy to Palóu and Crespí before the three came to America as Franciscan missionaries.

1797. In the vault farthest from the wall of the chancel were found the bones of Fr. Lasuén, who was interred there at the time of his death in 1803, according to the mission records. It was the vault nearest to the wall that presented problems. In that vault, above the disintegrating casket holding the remains of Fr. Lopez, was found a coffin of hexagonal shape in which there was a well-preserved skeleton. And outside this coffin were found the bones of a child. The hexagonal shape of the coffin dated it as having been placed there in the nineteenth century, and the well-preserved state of the skeletons showed that these were later burials.

The problem raised by these extra burials under the chancel floor was partly solved when Downie searched through the Carmel Book of Deaths which was preserved in the Chancery files in Diocesan headquarters. There he found an entry, number 2851, in which it was stated that on October 22, 1840 the body of Juan de la Guerray Carmella was taken from the San Carlos cemetery and placed in a sepulchre located on the gospel side of the church sanctuary. When Mrs. Goold heard of this, she told Downie that she had overheard her father speaking to her mother about the bodies of a child and a man in a black Spanish suit embroidered in gold thread that Fr. Casanova had seen when he opened the graves. Casanova had given the suit to her father, the caretaker, telling him to destroy it and to say nothing about these two extra bodies. There remained the mystery regarding the body of the child, but this was explained by the assumption that bereaved parents, natives of the region or squatters living nearby, had placed the body of their beloved in a place of special sanctity within the ruined walls of the church. The vault nearest the wall was probably chosen because it alone had a stone covering which could be easily removed for the child's burial.

In order that the identification of Serra's remains could be authenticated, two anthropologists were called to the scene, Dr. Theodore D. McCown, professor of anthropology at the

University of California, Berkeley, and Dr. Mark R. Harrington, curator of the Southwest Museum in Los Angeles. Of the undisturbed remains found in the coffin in the central vault, Dr. McCown wrote in his detailed report, "Tradition, historical fact, anthropology and archaeology combine overwhelmingly in establishing the identity of the cranium and skeleton of individual A . . . On the basis of historical evidence, the results of our anthropological enquiry and the facts recorded at the time of the exhumation, we can clearly identify individual A of grave B(2), the traditional Serra grave, as being the earthly remains of Father Junipero Serra."*

The final reinterments were made on December 7, 1943. The skeleton identified as that of Serra was arranged in a near natural position inside a new copper coffin which was placed in the central vault. The remains of López and Crespí were reinterred in new separate coffins in the first vault by the wall, while Lasuén's remains were placed in the vault next to the altar steps. Downie than cut identifying inscriptions in the cement covers of the vaults of the Franciscan padres and placed the remains of Juan de la Guerra and the child in a new vault which was made between the first vault and the rear wall of the sanctuary.

It was just three years after the definite identification of Serra's remains that there was returned to the Carmel church a carved figure that had been received by Serra in the earliest days of Mission San Carlos Borromeo. When the archbishop in Mexico City heard that José de Galvez was to sponsor an expedition for the exploration of Alta California, he presented him with a statue of Our Lady of Belen (Bethlehem) to be protector of the enterprise. Galvez entrusted the statue to Portolá, the leader of the exploration party, stating that Our Lady should be the *Conquistadora* of Nueva California. The

---

*Reported in "Where is Serra Buried?", an article by Fr. Raymond Geiger, O.F.M., in the *Provincial Annals XXVI,* January 1964, pp. 77-78.

The figure of Our Lady
of Belen above the altar
in the Belen (Bethlehem)
Chapel. (Courtesy of the
Downie Collection)

figure was taken north to Monterey Bay by Portolá and back
with him to Baja California. From there Galvez then sent it to
Serra to be placed in the Carmel mission church. That statue
occupied a place of honor in each of the successive churches of
the mission, finally being placed in the Belen Chapel of the
completed stone church.

When the Carmel mission was abandoned after secularization, the figure of Our Lady of Belen was entrusted to the last
native family to leave the mission. They carefully preserved it
in their home for many years. Years later the last member of
the family, Dona Maria Ignacia Dutra, enshrined the figure in
her home in Monterey. Dona Maria left it at her death to
Gertrude Ambrosio, who was a descendant of a Spanish
soldier in the first Portolá expedition; he had accompanied the
figure on its first journey to Monterey. Mrs. Ambrosio, who
was a member of the Carmel parish, returned the extant parts
of the ancient statue to the mission in 1948.

The lower part of the figure had disintegrated by the time it
came home to the mission church; only the head and hands

retained their original form and beauty. Downie carved a new torso to hold the clothing which he made from old vestments, a gold cope being used as an outer fall which paritally covered the dress. The child and the crown, parts of the original figure, he found among the relics stored at the Monterey church and returned them to their place with Our Lady. The handchased silver crown had been given by Naval Lieutenant Don Juan Bautista de Mutate in 1798 in fulfillment of a vow after his safe return from a dangerous voyage.

In completing the figure for installation again in the Belen Chapel, Downie made use of his own family possessions. His mother's hair was placed on the image of Our Lady and her locket was hung about the neck of the image of the infant. His grandmother's engagement ring was put upon Our Lady's hand. Downie then rebuilt and polychromed the figure of St. Joseph, which had also been given to the mission by Galvez, to stand with Our Lady in the Belen Chapel.

Sister Marie, in her thesis on the rebuilding of Mission San Carlos, includes a note which is worth repeating here. "Not only has Downie changed the placement of the statues in the church many times over," she reports, "but he has also changed their identity. He once converted this statue into Christ the King by nailing a sacred heart to the chest. Later he decided to remove the heart and restore the statue to its former state. The sudden conversion prompted a parishioner to command, 'Harry, stop changing the saints around. I never know which one I'm praying to.'"*

While he was busy restoring the mission as it had been in the past, Downie did not forget the current needs of the Carmel congregation. Though the natives who had filled the church in former times were accustomed to the chilly winter climate of the Carmel River area inside the church as well as out, modern worshippers prefer to pray in some degree of comfort. In order

---

*Quoted by Sister Marie in her thesis, page 68, footnote 11.

Heating pipes being installed in the floor of the Carmel mission church. (Courtesy of the Downie Collection)

that the Carmel church should be comfortable as well as beautiful, Downie oversaw the installation of heating pipes in the floor of the nave in 1946. The Franciscan padres of the eighteenth century would certainly have frowned upon such an addition, which they would have considered entirely unnecessary. But those attending services in the mission church in the twentieth century greatly appreciate this addition to the church's amenities.

Plans for a school to be housed in the buildings of the rebuilt mission compound had first been made in 1943 when the first classes were held in the Carmel summer house of the Sisters of Notre Dame. The school buildings were to be modern on the interior but were to have the outer appearance of the mission buildings as it was in the eighteenth century. By September 1945 the first of the schoolrooms in the reconstructed buildings of the compound were ready to receive pupils. The rooms grew along the south side of the patio as funds were available. The parish made annual contributions to the building fund as did such local money raising enterprises as the Bing Crosby

Golf Tournament at Pebble Beach. In 1950 that tournament contributed $5,000 to the drive for the $100,000 that was needed to complete the buildings.

In 1951 Crespí Hall was moved to its present location on Lasuén Road in order to make room for more classrooms and the school cafeteria along the west wing of the compound. In the next year the convent for the teaching Sisters of Notre Dame, built along Lasuén Road behind Crespí Hall, was dedicated. Today there are two hundred pupils in the Junipero Serra School, attending classes in rooms that are built upon the foundations first laid by Serra and his successors to house the California natives and to provide workshops for the mission enterprises.

The last addition to the buildings was made when the Munras Memorial Museum was built in the space left between Crespí Hall and the convent. Though this is properly out of the line of the original mission buildings, it is an important element of the tourist's visit to the mission. Here one can see a room furnished as it was in the days of the Spanish Dons of the Monterey Peninsula when this was the center of California life. On view in the main museum room are many interesting items

An air view of the nearly complete reconstruction of the Mission San Carlos Borromeo. (Courtesy of the Downie Collection)

preserved from the time of Spanish California which give an insight into the life of that time, including even a spoon that was found in the ruins of the Monterey Presidio after it was destroyed by the pirate Hippolyte Bouchard in 1818.

The museum was given by Lady Maria Antonia Field, a fourth generation member of the Munras family, one of the

Harry Downie and Lady Maria Antonia Field at the dedication of the Munras Memorial Museum. (Courtesy of the Downie Collection)

most prominent families of Monterey in the Spanish and Mexican periods. Lady Field, who was state secretary for the Mission Restoration Fund as early as 1919, joined Harry Downie, who had supervised the rebuilding of the mission since 1931, in the dedication of the museum building on September 20, 1961. Today's visitor to the mission views first the church building, then walks through the old cemetery beside the church in which hundreds of natives lie buried, to the back of the church where one enters the Munras Memorial

Museum to continue the journey in imagination back to the days of Colonial California.

The climax of the restoration of the Mission San Carlos Borromeo was reached when, on February 5, 1960, a Papal Bull was issued by Pope John XXIII granting the title of Basilica to this mission church. The term "basilica," which in Latin literature referred to any large roofed building that was dedicated to public use, has been adopted by the Catholic Church as a canonical title given to certain churches which are thereby endowed with special privileges. A Major Basilica is a papal church with a holy door and papal altar, while a Minor Basilica is a church of special historical and religious importance which takes precedence over all other churches but cathedrals. Mission San Carlos Borromeo church was made a Minor Basilica by the Papal Bull of February 1960.

Bishop Aloysius Willinger, Ordinary of the Diocese of Monterey-Fresno, had petitioned Archbishop Amleto Cicognani in 1954 for the designation of the Carmel mission church as a Minor Basilica, citing the importance of the mission in the history of the Catholic Church in California. In his request he noted that in this "cradle of California's faith" was to be found the burial place of Junípero Serra, founder of the California missions. Archbishop Cicognani agreed with the request and passed on the petition to the Vatican authorities. After years of careful investigation, the Congregation of Sacred Rites concurred in the request and recommended to the Pope that the petition be granted. With the issuing of the Papal Bull the Mission San Carlos Borromeo church became one of twelve Minor Basilicas in the United States.

Prior to the ceremony of the institution of the Basilica status, the great reredos had been raised behind the altar of the Carmel mission church. Carved and polychromed in the ancient manner by Harry Downie, it was made in the style of the reredos of Mission Dolores in San Francisco, where Harry had been nurtured in the faith. After studying the old records of the Carmel mission and the reports of those who had seen the church before secularization, he reconstructed the reredos to approximately the appearance of the one that had stood there before the destruction of the church interior after 1849.

In a framework of carved moldings and columns Downie placed the original statues that had been preserved in the Monterey parish through the years since secularization. At the top, below the dove representing the Holy Spirit, is to be seen the figure of San Carlos Borromeo, the patron saint of the mission. On the left side, as one faces the altar, have been placed the figures of St. Michael Archangel and of the Virgin Mary, standing for *Ave Maria Purisima* (Hail Mary Most Pure). To the right, the statue of St. Anthony of Padua stands above that of St. Bonaventura. At each side of the large crucifix above the altar are the figures of Mary and St. John. It was fitting that the reredos which served to complete the mission church as it was in the days of greatest glory should have been completed and in place for the ceremony which marked the Carmel mission's greatest honor.

The cermony of the institution of the Minor Basilica began at the diocesan headquarters in Fresno on April 26, 1962, where Bishop Willinger conducted a pontifical mass in the Civic Auditorium in the presence of James Cardinal McIntyre and Archbishop Egidio Vagnozzi, the Apostolic Delegate to the United States. That evening there was a banquet in honor of Bishop Willinger, and the next morning the visiting prelates and others taking part in the ceremonies were taken by bus through Pacheco Pass and the Salinas Valley to Carmel.

At four o'clock in the afternoon on April 27, the ceremonies began at Carmel with a formal procession in which were carried the two basilica symbols which had been created for the occasion, the Tintanablum, a bell in a carved and poly-chromed stand which is a symbol of the bell that was rung when the Pope approached a basilica church, and the Cana-poeum, an umbrella-type symbol that represents the tent that was set up outside the church, to be used as the Papal vesting room. These basilica symbols were then set up on either side of the altar for the institution ceremonies. The reading of the Papal Bull was followed by a pontifical mass celebrated by James Cardinal McIntyre. The Paulist Choir from San Francisco was accompanied in the music for the ceremonies by the brass section of the Monterey Peninsula College orchestra. The congregation filled the church and the forecourt, where the service was carried by the public address system installed for the occasion.

The two symbols of the Minor Basilica are to be seen today extending from the right and left walls of the church just inside the main door, where they have been placed for permanent

James Cardinal McIntyre celebrating mass on the occasion of the institution of the Carmel mission as a minor basilica. (Courtesy of the Downie Collection)

display. To the left is the Tintanablum with the bell suspended within the stand carved by Downie. To the right is the Canapoeum, also created at Carmel. Each section of the umbrella-tent contains embroidered designs to represent the heritage of this Basilica church. The coat of arms of the Carmelite Order, for which the river and area are named, is represented on the first panel on the altar side of the Canapoeum. On the next has been embroidered the form of a cardinal's hat for St. Charles Borromeo, the patron saint of the mission. There follows then a combination of symbols to represent Junípero Serra—an old fashioned saw, because *serra* means a saw in Spanish, and a hammer to stand for his mother's surname, Herrero, blacksmith in Spanish. In the fourth panel there are representations of a carpenter's square and a lily for St. Joseph, to whom the church itself is dedicated.*

The Basilica welcomes more than two hundred thousand visitors each year who come to view what is considered by many to be the most beautiful mission in California and is recognized by all to be the most perfectly restored. The present church building within its original stone walls, appearing today as it did when it was filled with the first natives of the Carmel River Valley, stands as a living witness to the faith of those who founded it, preserved it, and rebuilt it for the use of present and future generations.

---

*The figure of St. Joseph is generally represented with him holding his staff topped with a lily blossom, from the story that when he doubted Mary's purity, his staff stuck in the ground bloomed, to show him that Mary was indeed a pure virgin though she carried a child within her.

## Bibliographical Notes

The only written record of the rebuilding of the Carmel mission under the supervision of Harry Downie is to be found in *The Restoration of Mission San Carlos Borromeo, California, 1931-1967*, a thesis presented to the faculty of the history department of the University of San Francisco by Sister Marie Celeste Pagliarulo, S.N.D., June 1968. Copies of this thesis, which is based on interviews with Downie by Sister Marie in 1966 and 1967 plus all pertinent sources that she could find, are to be found in the Harry Downie Library of the Carmel mission and in the library of the University of San Francisco.

# Index